Advanced Introduction to Business Ethics

Elgar Advanced Introductions are stimulating and thoughtful introductions to major fields in the social sciences, business and law, expertly written by the world's leading scholars. Designed to be accessible yet rigorous, they offer concise and lucid surveys of the substantive and policy issues associated with discrete subject areas.

The aims of the series are two-fold: to pinpoint essential principles of a particular field, and to offer insights that stimulate critical thinking. By distilling the vast and often technical corpus of information on the subject into a concise and meaningful form, the books serve as accessible introductions for undergraduate and graduate students coming to the subject for the first time. Importantly, they also develop well-informed, nuanced critiques of the field that will challenge and extend the understanding of advanced students, scholars and policy-makers.

For a full list of titles in the series please see the back of the book. Recent titles in the series include:

Advanced Introduction to

Business Ethics

JOHN HOOKER

T. Jerome Holleran Professor of Business Ethics and Social Responsibility and Professor of Operations Research, Tepper School of Business, Carnegie Mellon University, USA

Elgar Advanced Introductions

Edward Elgar
PUBLISHING

Cheltenham, UK • Northampton, MA, USA

Published by
Edward Elgar Publishing Limited
The Lypiatts
15 Lansdown Road
Cheltenham
Glos GL50 2JA
UK

Edward Elgar Publishing, Inc.
William Pratt House
9 Dewey Court
Northampton
Massachusetts 01060
USA

A catalogue record for this book
is available from the British Library

Library of Congress Control Number: 2021939231

ISBN 978 1 80037 855 1 (cased)
ISBN 978 1 80037 857 5 (paperback)
ISBN 978 1 80037 856 8 (eBook)

Printed and bound in Great Britain by TJ Books Limited, Padstow, Cornwall

Contents

1   Why business ethics?

Building consensus

Ethics is the way we reach consensus on how we are to live and work together. Without ethics, society would promptly descend into intolerable chaos. Without business ethics in particular, commerce as we know it would collapse.

It is often assumed that laws and regulations carry the burden of maintaining social order. Yet they, too, rest on ethics. Suppose, for example, that everyone starts ignoring traffic signals tomorrow morning. There are not nearly enough police officers to patrol every intersection and put a stop to it. Even if intersections are surveilled by cameras, officials would be overwhelmed by the task of scanning the images and sending citations to millions of violators. In any event, an unethical public could simply ignore the citations. Overburdened traffic courts cannot even begin to issue arrest warrants to an entire motoring population.

Or suppose that tonight, people begin breaking into thousands of houses and apartments. The police cannot be everywhere at once. Even if law enforcement in such a scenario were possible, an unethical police force could look the other way or take bribes. In anything short of an oppressive police state, and perhaps even there, law enforcement is powerless to maintain order without largely voluntary compliance.

It is the same in the business world. Governments can issue regulations but have nowhere near the staffing level necessary to enforce them, if companies choose not to comply. Even when enforcement is possible, clever business managers can stay a step ahead of regulations, particularly in today's complex and fast-moving commercial environment. One might suppose that reputational effects can incentivize ethical conduct, since unscrupulous businesses will lose customers in a competitive market. Yet even if we grant that market incentives alone can govern a complex economy, the very possibility of a competitive market relies on a pre-disposition to be ethical. If merchants routinely fail to deliver what is promised and customers routinely fail to pay what they owe, there can be no meaningful competition. Commerce, like society in general, rests on largely voluntary compliance with ethical norms.

The field of ethics offers a path to voluntary compliance by seeking rational consensus on what the norms should be. People are not likely to conform to behavioral norms unless they basically agree with them. Most of us obey traffic signals, even when the police are not looking, because we know that they are necessary to manage traffic. We refrain from burglarizing homes, because we recognize at some level that a secure home is necessary for civilized life. Business people, by and large, conduct their affairs in good faith, because they know that the profitability of their enterprise relies on an orderly and predictable commercial environment. The business world, and society in general, work to the extent they do because we have reached consensus on such matters.

Ethics supplies the intellectual equipment for negotiating this consensus. It is true that common sense suffices in many cases. One need not study Aristotle or Kant to realize that widespread burglary is a bad idea. But today's complex society poses ethical dilemmas that require deep analysis. When should governments permit immigrants or refugees to enter the country? Should social media sites allow false or incendiary material to be posted? When should life support be withdrawn from a terminally ill patient? Business dilemmas are no less vexing. What is a fair price for a successful drug, given the high cost of research and clinical trials? Can a bakery ethically refuse to cater a gay wedding? Is it ethical for a manufacturer to destroy a local economy by moving its operations to a low-wage country? Should a company harvest and sell customer data? Should employers provide paid sick leave, even when not required by law? These and many other dilemmas urgently require convincing answers, which in turn require careful and clear-headed analysis.

Finding objectivity in ethics

A major obstacle to ethical reasoning is the widespread assumption that there is no objectivity in the field. There are empirical methods for resolving questions in physics and biology, but ethics is seen as just a matter of personal opinion. Some even believe that we *should* regard ethics as just a matter of opinion, or else people will impose their values on others.

There appear to be several reasons for this skepticism. A primary reason is that very few people have ever seen a rigorous ethical argument. I myself did not see one until I was in graduate school. So it is no surprise that one might believe that close reasoning is impossible in ethics. Another factor is the historical fashion in which we are exposed to the field, when we are exposed at all. We are taught the very different ethical systems of Plato, Aristotle, Thomas Aquinas, Bentham, Kant, and so forth, which gives the impression that there can be no consensus in ethics. It would be like teaching physics by taking students through the historical theories of Ptolemy, Copernicus, Newton, Einstein, and Heisenberg, which seem equally incommensurate.

A further reason for the apparent lack of consensus is that many if not most ethical thinkers have primarily occupied themselves with the philosophy of ethics (also known as *metaethics*) rather than ethics proper. Metaethics is concerned with how ethical propositions can be understood and justified, rather than which ones are actually true. The dominance of metaethics is so strong in the academic literature that one must speak of *normative ethics*, rather than simply ethics, to make clear that one is interested in questions of right and wrong. Philosophical discussion thrives on controversy and disparate viewpoints, and we should expect nothing different in metaethics. In normative ethics, however, the aim is the opposite: to arrive at rational consensus. This is what we see in the sciences, where nearly all scientific thinkers are scientists rather than philosophers of science. This book is dedicated to (normative) ethics, to distinguishing right from wrong, much as a textbook in science is dedicated primarily to science rather than the philosophy of science.

Popular skepticism notwithstanding, objectivity is possible in ethics. It is not achieved as in the natural or social sciences, because ethics is not an empirical field. It does not establish principles by collecting data or performing experiments. The methodology is more like that of mathematics, which is based on proof techniques for deducing conclusions from axioms. Mathematical proof techniques include proof by contradiction, proof by mathematical induction, proof by construction, probabilistic methods, and combinatorial arguments. In ethics, the axioms are the necessary conditions for the possibility of freely chosen action. The proof techniques consist of applying general principles that can be derived from these conditions, a task that can require ingenuity and careful thought, much as in mathematics. Three such principles form the core of this book: the *generalization principle*, the *utilitarian principle*, and the *autonomy principle*. One may ask, why three? Why not two or four? One might also ask why there are five mathematical proof techniques. It is because, over the centuries, mathematicians have stumbled across these five and found them to be useful. The situation is similar in ethics.

To be sure, deductive reasoning in ethics does not offer the same degree of certainty, or achieve consensus as reliably, as it does in mathematics. This is because ethics is harder than mathematics (I know, because I am an applied mathematician). Ethics must deal with life in general rather than just quantifiable aspects of the world. Yet we can obtain a certain degree of objectivity in ethics if we put our minds to it. Too often, we want ethics to be easy. We want to be able to rely on gut feeling or a few common-sense rules. Yet consider how much hard work and brilliance have been necessary to make progress in mathematics. Ethics requires nothing less. Fortunately, the field benefits from some of the smartest thinkers who ever walked the earth: Socrates, Aristotle, Confucius, Mencius, Siddhārtha Gautama (the Buddha), Adi Shankara, Thomas Aquinas, Immanuel Kant, John Stuart Mill, and a number of more recent luminaries. By distilling insights and ideas from this grand tradition, we can make progress in ethics.

An alternative, non-deductive method of ethical reasoning is frequently employed in the normative ethics literature. Generally attributed to John Rawls (1951, 1971) and in a more general context to Nelson Goodman (1955), it strives for a *reflective equilibrium* using a process somewhat analogous to empirical inquiry. An ethical principle is proposed and then applied in thought experiments to various specific situations. If the principle calls for behavior that seems wrong in some of these situations, it is revised to eliminate the counterintuitive outcomes, and again tested in thought experiments. The process continues until an equilibrium of principles and case-specific intuitions is reached. A key element of this method is concocting situations in enough realistic detail to allow one's ethical intuitions to operate properly. These intuitions serve as "data" that experimentally confirm or refute an ethical claim.

This book scrupulously avoids reliance on reflective equilibrium. It never defends an ethical conclusion on the ground that it seems intuitively plausible, for two reasons. An obvious one is that different people often have different intuitions, particularly when we most urgently need to build consensus. Suppose that an apparel firm proposes to reduce production costs by sourcing tennis shoes from low-wage sweatshops overseas. A manager and a labor activist may have very different intuitions about the ethics of this practice (Meyers, 2004). The manager will point out that sweatshops offer better pay than is otherwise available locally, and sourcing from them is therefore perfectly ethical. The labor activist will insist that exploiting workers who struggle with poverty is clearly wrong, particularly when manufacturing accounts for a tiny fraction of the retail price of shoes. Consensus on the issue remains elusive.

A deeper problem with reflective equilibrium is that one's ethical intuitions in a thought experiment are, at best, a reflection of current social norms rather than what is actually right or wrong. Social norms can be confusing and inconsistent, not to mention grievously wrong, as witnessed by the fact that many societies have viewed slavery as acceptable. Intuitions can play a legitimate role in ethics, much as they do in mathematics, where they suggest interesting conjectures that one might attempt to prove. But the intuitions themselves carry no epistemic weight. Only reasoned argument can settle the matter.

Finally, there is the concern, mentioned earlier, that viewing ethics as objective will encourage people to impose their values on others. This misunderstands the role and purpose of ethics. The whole point of ethics, as developed here, is to arrive at a rational *consensus* on values—to reach agreement on ethical norms so that we will all adhere to them voluntarily, rather than impose them on others.

What about unethical behavior?

It may appear that the main problem in ethics is getting people to behave ethically, not determining what is ethical. Corporate ethics scandals are constantly in the news, and business people must frequently deal with unscrupulous co-workers, bosses, or subordinates. This may suggest that ethics books like this one should focus on how to influence human behavior, not how to analyze ethical issues.

There is, in fact, a sizeable research literature on behavioral ethics, which seeks psychological and sociological explanations for unethical conduct (Mitchell et al., 2020). Yet there are two problems with viewing ethics solely from a behavioral perspective. One is that we cannot recognize unethical behavior in the first place unless we know what is ethical. As already observed, this is a constant challenge. Another is that, more often than we realize, people go astray because they cannot identify the ethical path. This is particularly true in organizations, where it is often difficult to sort out the issues when one is immersed in the complexity of a real-world dilemma. Even if some members of the organization can identify the right course of action, they may lack the vocabulary or conceptual framework to challenge colleagues who persuasively argue for the opposite position. After all, people have a strong tendency to believe they are in the right. Even terrorists are convinced that their cause is just.

A glimpse at two case studies

Two case studies illustrate the importance of ethical competence in organizations, even though a full analysis of them must be postponed to Chapter 4. The first case study, one of the most famous in the ethics literature, shows how well-intentioned managers can easily arrive at the wrong conclusion. It dates from the 1970s but it is particularly valuable because we have an insider's account of the decision process. The second, more recent case study shows how vexing and unobvious an ethical choice can be.

Ford Motor Company's budget car of the 1970s, the Pinto, had a problem with exploding fuel tanks. A protruding stud from the rear axle could penetrate the tank during a low-speed collision and trigger a conflagration. Ford determined that it could recall the car for repairs and fix the defect for a cost of $11 per car. It decided against the recall. Distressingly, reports of fiery explosions continued to come in. After three teenage girls were incinerated in a much-publicized tragedy, Ford executives were criminally prosecuted in 1978 for reckless homicide and narrowly escaped conviction. The company shortly thereafter recalled the defective cars for repairs.

Dennis Gioia was a young manager in the recall division at Ford. He published an honest and courageous article about the Pinto case some years later, after he had become a business school professor (Gioia, 1992). He writes in the article that he took the job at Ford with the ambition of making a positive contribution to the world. Upon receiving reports of Pinto fuel tank explosions, he and his colleagues performed a cost–benefit analysis. They found that the cost of fixing 12.5 million cars would amount to $137 million, whereas the benefit of doing so would come to only about $49.5 million. The latter figure was based on avoiding a projected 180 deaths at $200,000 per death, 180 projected burn injuries at $67,000 per injury, and 2100 burned cars at $700 per car. Since this calculation took into account the welfare of everyone concerned, not just the company, the team was ethically comfortable with deciding against a recall. Gioia reports in his article that he continued to defend this decision for some years while discussing the case study in his classes. He eventually changed his mind but does not explain why.

Ford's decision was unethical, but not, as one might think, because it placed a monetary value on human life. This is done routinely and is unavoidable. If a city budget is based on the assumption that human life is infinitely valuable, it will devote all funds to traffic safety and none to schools. Indeed, we implicitly assign a monetary value to our own lives. If I have the option of buying a car with a safety feature that reduces the chances of a traffic fatality by 1 in 1000, then I must decide how much I would be willing to pay for the option. That amount, multiplied by 1000, is the value I assign to my life. Chapter 4 will identify the flaw in Ford's reasoning, after the necessary conceptual equipment is at hand, but one can observe now that its ethical lapse was not due to bad people. On the contrary, it was the result of well-intentioned managers lacking the tools to analyze the issue properly. Even Gioia's change of mind, years later, appears to have no rational grounding. This is a recipe for bad decisions.

Guidant Corporation, now part of Boston Scientific, was the first company to produce implantable defibrillators for heart patients. One of its devices was implanted in a young man, Joshua, who died of heart failure on a cycling trip (Sandbu and Wen, 2008). An autopsy revealed that the defibrillator had malfunctioned due to a defect that Guidant had known about for some time. Guidant had not notified doctors or patients, although it did report the defect to the United States (U.S.) Food and Drug Administration, as required by law. It had also promptly corrected the problem in new devices. In the meantime, Guidant was negotiating a buyout by Johnson & Johnson, and publicity about the defect would have resulted in a smaller offer. As it happened, a *New York Times* reporter (Meyer, 2005) got wind of the story and published it under the headline, "Maker of Heart Device Kept Flaw from Doctors," whereupon the buyout fell through.

When Joshua's doctors learned about Guidant's secrecy, they were furious. They insisted that they would have replaced the device if only they had known it was defective. Joshua's father lamented, "Whoever made this decision at Guidant, I pray he doesn't have a son who this happens to."

Guidant had a medical justification for its decision: it was more dangerous to replace a defective device than not to do so. Replacement carried a 0.42 percent risk of death, while leaving the device in place incurred only a 0.1 to 0.24 percent lethal risk. Guidant probably reasoned that doctors and patients would be eager to replace a device with a known defect, as in Joshua's case. Since some 41,000 implants had been performed, this would have resulted in 75 to 130 unnecessary deaths. It was just for this reason that the Food and Drug Administration did not require companies to publicize defects of this kind. Yet Guidant's argument was met with fierce opposition. One of Joshua's doctors remarked, "It is a statistical argument that has little to do with real people." Worse, Guidant's inaction looked like a crass business decision, due to the financial conflict of interest with the proposed buyout.

Actually, Guidant's decision may well have been the ethical one. We must again postpone a detailed discussion until we are ready for it, but one point is already clear. Business dilemmas can be difficult and even excruciating. Well-intentioned managers can easily make ethical mistakes, and they can be excoriated even when they are right. Personal feelings and moral intuitions cannot resolve such matters. Only reasoned argument stands a chance.

Fiduciary duty

Business ethics is frequently identified with *fiduciary duty*, conceived as an obligation to promote the financial interests of company owners or stockholders. On this view, the sole obligation of business managers is to maximize profit for shareholders, subject to legal constraints. If this is true, there is no need for ethics books like this one, only for business know-how. Yet this reductionist theory is implausible on its face, because it imposes ethical duties only when there are shareholders. If one is a sole proprietor, one can presumably maximize profits by any legal means without worrying about ethics. It is a philosophy an Ebenezer Scrooge might love.

The single-minded focus on shareholder value originated in the academic literature, not the business world. An influential article by Michael Jensen and William Meckling (1976) in the *Journal of Financial Economics* argued for the primacy of stockholder interests on economic and financial grounds. The article enhanced the academic respectability of views already expressed by economist Milton Friedman in his famous *New York Times Magazine* article (1970), where he claims that a company's only responsibility is to its stockholders. Friedman's article, in turn, echoes his book *Capitalism and Freedom* (1962), which contains his much-quoted remark, "there is one and only one social responsibility of business—to use its resources and engage in activities designed to increase its profits so long as it stays within the rules of the game, which is to say, engages in open and free competition without deception or fraud" (p. 55).

Fiduciary duty certainly exists when a firm has stockholders. It can be based on an agency agreement between the stockholders on the one hand and managers and members of the board of directors on the other. The manager and board members promise to seek financial returns on behalf of stockholders, in exchange for salaries and bonuses. There is generally an ethical duty to keep one's promises, and there is no obvious reason why the fiduciary promise should be an exception. Yet two basic questions remain:

a. Are there ethical obligations beyond fiduciary duty?
b. How far must one go to honor the fiduciary promise?

Friedman himself opens the door to obligations beyond fiduciary duty when he rules out deception and fraud. In his magazine article he says further that managers should "make as much money as possible" for shareholders "while conforming to their basic rules of the society, both those embodied in law and those embodied in ethical custom." This already backs away significantly from reductionist business ethics, since basic rules of society and ethical custom cover a wide range of obligations beyond fiduciary duty. Yet it raises the question as to how to identify ethical custom. Business dilemmas tend to arise precisely when social norms are unclear or controversial. One may also question why only rules recognized by society should be considered. If we say that ethics is nothing more than "ethical custom," Friedman's position reduces to the useless and tautological claim that maximizing profit is ethical except when it is not ethical.

Stakeholder theory offers a clear alternative to reductionist business ethics by answering question (a) strongly in the affirmative. It extends a company's obligations to include to all "stakeholders," not just stockholders. Generally credited to Ian Mitroff (1983) and R. Edward Freeman (1983), stakeholder theory asks a business to consider the interests of employees, customers, suppliers, the surrounding community, and other affected parties in their decision making. A large literature has grown around this perspective, but it is unclear how the concept of stakeholder obligation, in and of itself, provides a clue as to how to balance competing obligations toward the various stakeholders. It also raises what is known as the *stakeholder paradox*: we are forced to choose between "business without ethics" and "ethics without business." Maximizing shareholder value is business without ethics, while an imperative to consider all stakeholders recognizes no special obligation to shareholders. Without this special obligation, the business is arguably not a business but a social service agency.

Kenneth Goodpaster (1991) addressed the stakeholder paradox by pro-posing that firms have a different kind of obligation to stockholders than to stakeholders in general. The duty to stockholders is fiduciary, because it is based on a promise as described above. The duty to stakeholders in general is to consider the impact of business decisions on their welfare, but the duty is not based on a promise. This may resolve the paradox to an extent, but question (b) raised above remains: what exactly does the promise to stockholders entail? In particular, does it require neglecting the interests of other stakeholders when they conflict with profitability?

A straightforward approach to this question, and the one adopted in this book, begins by recalling that fiduciaries act on behalf of owners; they are agents for the owners. The owners cannot ethically ask fiduciaries to do on their behalf what would be unethical for the owners to do themselves. An organized crime boss cannot escape responsibility for murder by hiring someone else to do it, and it is no different for business decisions. This makes the obligations of owners the primary issue in business ethics.[1] If it is ethical and profitable for owners to devastate the local economy by offshoring a factory to Vietnam, then it is ethical for fiduciaries to do it on their behalf. If it is not ethical for owners, then it is not ethical for fiduciaries to do it on their behalf. While fiduciaries have promised to act in the financial interests of owners, the promise does not require them to take unethical steps to do so. We will see in Chapter 3 that there is a logical contradiction in the very notion of promising to carry out an unethical action.

This approach dissolves the issue of how to balance obligations to owners against obligations to other stakeholders. Rather, it asks what obligations the owners have to the various stakeholders. This question, in turn, is addressed by ethical analysis in general, such as the kind of analysis carried out in this book. Fiduciary duty therefore becomes a secondary concern. It arises only if there are stockholders in the first place, and only after one has determined what actions are ethical for owners themselves to take. This is almost always the more substantive and difficult question from an ethical standpoint.

---

[1]   In this context, "owners" need not literally be holders of company shares, but any group of investors or other persons to whom the board members and managers can be seen as owing a fiduciary obligation based on an agency agreement.

Ethics and self-interest

Even if one accepts that the primary issue in business ethics is the duty of owners, one can still maintain that these owners ought to pursue self-interest by maximizing profit. This view usually takes two forms. One is *ethical egoism*, which holds that one's sole ethical duty is to pursue one's own interests, which presumably implies that business owners have no obligation beyond legally obtained profit. The other is *psychological egoism*, which holds that people are going to pursue their self-interest whether moralists like it or not. Either view implies, again, that ethics books like this one are unnecessary. We need only books on business management and perhaps business law.

The egoist perspective is popularly associated with Adam Smith, in what is probably one of the more egregious misinterpretations of a historical thinker on record. We are constantly reminded of Smith's remark in *The Wealth of Nations* that by pursuing self-interest, the merchant is "led by an invisible hand to promote an end which was no part of his intention," namely the "public interest" (1776, book 4, chapter 2, paragraph 9). This presumably implies that self-interest is good and should regulate business behavior. Economists love to quote his statement, "It is not from the benevolence of the butcher, the brewer, or the baker that we expect our dinner, but from their regard to their own self-interest" (1776, book 1, chapter 2, paragraph 2). Taken out of context, this could be read as a full-throated endorsement of psychological egoism.

Due to Smith's influence on how we think about business ethics, it is important to clarify what he actually said. First, we note that he was, in fact, an ethicist, not an economist in the modern sense. He occupied the Chair in Moral Philosophy at the University of Glasgow, which was established in 1727 and still exists today. As for psychological egoism, he explicitly rejected it. Inspired by his mentor Francis Hutcheson, a prior occupant of the ethics chair and a seminal figure in the Scottish Enlightenment, Smith saw human beings as strongly motivated by empathy as well as self-interest. Smith's book *The Theory of Moral Sentiments* (1759) develops this thesis, beginning with its very first sentence. Lest anyone think that he moved beyond this opinion when he wrote *The Wealth of Nations*, he revised *The Theory of Moral Sentiments* several times, last doing so shortly before his death in 1790. It evidently represents his final views on

WHY BUSINESS ETHICS?   13

the matter. As for ethical egoism, he rejected it as well. He believed that right and wrong should be based on the moral intuitions of an impartial observer, who would be motivated by empathy as well as self-interest.

We should also examine the contexts from which the famous quotes are extracted. The passage about the invisible hand is part of Smith's case against mercantilism. He argued that there was no need for protectionist restrictions on international trade, because it was (at that time) in the interest of merchants to conduct most of their business domestically anyway. Thus if merchants were allowed to pursue their self-interest, they would give priority to the domestic economy as though "led by an invisible hand." Smith was therefore proposing an approach to managing international trade, not a general principle of allowing self-interest to govern an economy. In fact, Smith favored a certain amount of government regulation as well as progressive taxation. The remarks about the butcher, brewer and baker occur in Smith's discussion of how the division of labor leads to trade. When we specialize, we must obtain most of what we need from others. Smith observes that we are generally more likely to obtain our meat, beer and bread by exchanging something for them rather than relying solely on the generosity of those who produce them. This rather obvious point falls far short of psychological egoism.

The appeal of psychological egoism, aside from conveniently justifying selfish behavior, seems to stem from the tautological way it is formulated. Obvious examples of generosity and self-sacrifice are explained away by claiming that they actually meet hidden psychological needs. Nothing is allowed to count against psychological egoism, which therefore loses all content. If we avoid this self-defeating maneuver, we discover that purely altruistic behavior is prevalent and well documented. A remarkable volume by Matthieu Ricard (2015) fills 864 pages with scientific evidence for altruism in humans and other animals. Business people, in particular, often find meaning in their work by making a contribution to society beyond that incentivized by personal returns.

Moving to ethical egoism, it might be defended on the grounds that the legal pursuit of pure self-interest motivates people to work hard and create more wealth. Society as a whole therefore supposedly benefits more when business people focus exclusively on the legal pursuit of profit. There are two major problems with this line of argument. First, the premise that unfettered self-interest best benefits society is a sweeping claim that requires empirical evidence. One thinks, for example, of Turing Pharmaceuticals chief executive officer (CEO) Martin Shkreli's notorious decision to raise the price of Daraprim from $13.50 to $750 per pill overnight (Pollack, 2015). The drug had been used to treat malaria and other conditions for over 60 years. While the extreme price hike was perfectly legal and served the interests of company executives and stockholders, the benefit to society at large was much less clear.

Second, even if it could be established that pure profit maximization benefits society, any ethical conclusions require further argument. We will find that while there is an obligation to promote overall welfare, the means to do so must satisfy other ethical principles. Business decisions must therefore be ethically evaluated case by case. It is much too early to announce, with a wave of the hand, that business should be entirely governed by an overarching principle of legal profit maximization.

2 Facts, values, and reason

Facts and values

The first step toward objective resolution of ethical issues is to distinguish facts from values. Facts are observable states of affairs, while values have to do with what is right or wrong, good or bad. The fact/value distinction will enter into nearly every issue examined in this book. It is a vital distinction because values, and ethical obligations in particular, can never be inferred from facts alone. One must apply ethical principles. Ethical principles, in turn, are derived from two basic assumptions about the nature of reason: free actions must be based on reasons, and reason is universal. Because these assumptions underlie all ethical arguments in the book, they are examined carefully in subsequent sections of this chapter.

The gulf separating facts and values is commonly referred to as the *is-ought gap*, first clearly described by David Hume in his brilliant essay, *A Treatise of Human Nature* (1739). Hume insisted that one cannot infer what ought to be solely from what is. For example, one cannot infer that cheating on an exam is OK by observing that everyone else in the class is cheating, because what others are doing is purely a matter of fact. Any such inference requires an ethical premise, such as the assertion that it is permissible to do what everyone else is doing. Not even the fact that bombing a train station will kill innocent people implies, in and of itself, that one should not bomb a train station. One needs the additional premise that it is wrong to kill innocent people.

Two centuries after Hume, G. E. Moore (1903) defended the is-ought gap with a simple argument. Even if one grants that everyone is cheating, one can still sensibly *ask* whether cheating is wrong. Even if one grants that bombing a train station will take innocent lives, one can still raise the issue, without contradicting oneself, as to whether bombing a train station is wrong (terrorists claim it is not wrong). The assertion that it is wrong must therefore have content that goes beyond the facts. To jump directly from facts to ethics is, according to Moore, to commit the *naturalistic fallacy*—to ground ethics solely in nature.[1]

This is not academic hairsplitting. The naturalistic fallacy can have, and has had, major consequences in the business world. Industrialist Andrew Carnegie was much taken with the ideas of nineteenth-century philosopher Herbert Spencer, who is famous for coining the phrase "survival of the fittest" to describe Darwinian evolution (Spencer, 1864). Carnegie saw this natural process as justifying the shockingly high fatality rate in his steel mills. He even invited Spencer to Pittsburgh to witness how he was weeding out the weak, thus improving the species. Spencer was repulsed by the spectacle (Wall, 1989), but industrialists of the era continued to seek justification in his ideas.

The naturalistic fallacy is by no means confined to the nineteenth century. We continue to see efforts to reduce ethics to facts. One well-known example is the concept of sociobiology promoted by Edward O. Wilson, who claimed that ethics should be "biologicized" (1975, p. 27). Another example occurs in Chapter 1, which noted a widespread tendency to justify legal profit maximization on the grounds that it (allegedly) maximizes overall welfare. This is again an instance of the naturalistic fallacy, unless it is based on an ethical premise as well. For example, one might claim that actions maximizing overall welfare are necessarily ethical. Yet this ethical premise becomes less plausible when it is explicitly stated and examined. Overall welfare might be maximized, for example, by neglecting those with mental and physical impairments.

Chapter 1 also noted the very different ways in which facts and values are established. Facts are revealed only by empirical observation, and ethical

---

[1]   The dominant tradition in naturalistic ethics is virtue ethics, or natural law theory, which has roots in Aristotle and is associated with Thomas Aquinas. Virtue ethics experienced a revival in the twentieth century, led by such thinkers as G. E. M. Anscombe (1958), Bernard Williams (1985), and Alistair MacIntyre (1985). An overview of this work can be found in Trianosky (1997 [1990]). Extended critical discussions of virtue ethics are provided by Gilbert Harman (1977, 1999, 2003).

principles only by deductive reasoning. This distinction has enormous practical implications when we discuss ethical issues with our colleagues. Disputes often boil down to disagreement on the facts, and no amount of debate can establish the facts. To make progress, we must stop talking and start investigating the world. On the other hand, no amount of empirical research will resolve disagreements on ethical norms. Only ethical analysis can resolve the issue. Analysis is also necessary to determine which facts are relevant to the ethical question. To sum up:

- *Ethics cannot tell us the facts.* We must go out and gather data. No amount of talk will settle issues of fact.
- *Facts alone cannot tell us what is ethical.* We must arrive at the relevant principles by deductive reasoning.
- *Ethics can tell us which facts matter.* This can save a great deal of effort, because we can chase down only the facts that are relevant to the issue at hand.

Acting for reasons

Ethical principles can be derived from two basic assumptions. One is the assumption that when one *acts*, one acts for a *reason*. In this context, a reason is understood to be a rationale that one consciously takes as justifying the action, not a biological cause or psychological motivation. Behavior for which one lacks such a reason is *mere behavior*, rather than freely chosen action. If I hiccup, there is a reason for it in the sense of a gastric cause, but it is mere behavior, because I have no conscious rationale for it. On the other hand, if I take a drink of water to stop the hiccups, this is an action because I deliberately perform it for a reason. Thus an action has two kinds of explanation, a conscious rationale as well as a biological/psychological cause, whereas mere behavior has only the latter kind of explanation. The rationale need not offer a good or convincing reason for the action, but only serve as an *intelligible explanation* for why I deliberately undertook the action. The explanation must be intelligible, because an explanation no one can understand is not an explanation.

A being who is capable of freely chosen action is an *agent* (sometimes called a *moral agent*), and taking action is an exercise of *agency*. The connection between agency and reasons is deeply embedded in the philosophical tradition, having origins in the work of Aristotle and Kant, and reinforced in more recent times by the writings of G. E. M. Anscombe (1958), Donald Davidson (1963), and others. The idea that action, unlike mere behavior, has two kinds of explanation has roots in Kant, who suggested that an action can be viewed from two standpoints: as part of the natural realm of cause and effect, and as part of a "world of understanding" in which actions have a rationale.[2] This *dual standpoint theory* was a groundbreaking concept that allowed ethics to move beyond a seeming conflict between free will and determinism. Even though actions are physically determined, they can nonetheless be assessed ethically because they must have an intelligible explanation. In fact, *ethical principles are nothing more than necessary conditions for the intelligibility of the explanation.*

Universality of reason

A second basic assumption for ethical analysis is the *universality of reason*. This is basically the principle that while we have a right to our own opinion, we do not have a right to our own logic. If a reason justifies a conclusion for me, then it justifies that conclusion for anyone; reason is the same regardless of who does the reasoning. This is a postulate behind all intellectual inquiry. In ethics, it says that if a reason justifies an action for me, then it justifies the same action for anyone else to whom the reason applies. Either the reason justifies the action or it does not, and if it

---

[2]   In Kant's words, "Der Begriff einer Verstandeswelt is also nur ein *Standpunkt*, den die Vernunft sich genöthigt sieht, außer den Erscheinungen zu nehmen, um *sich selbst als praktisch zu denken*" (Kant, 1785, p. 458, original emphasis), or, "the concept of a world of understanding is therefore only a *standpoint* that reason sees itself constrained to take outside of appearances [i.e., outside the world of cause and effect] *in order to think of itself as practical* [i.e., in order to think of itself as taking action]." In recent times, variations of the dual standpoint theory have been developed by Nagel (1986), Korsgaard (1996), Nelkin (2000), and Bilgrami (2006).

justifies the action, then it justifies the action whether or not one happens to have my name and address.

Suppose I open my umbrella when the rain starts, for two reasons: I happen to have an umbrella, and because I do not like getting wet. Then I am committed to saying that anyone who has an umbrella when the rain starts, and does not like getting wet, should open the umbrella. Someone else may enjoy walking in the rain and neglect to open the umbrella for that reason. But if this is so, my reasons do not apply, and I am not recommending umbrella use to that person. Still others may be walking in wind that is too strong for an umbrella, and I certainly do not want to recommend using one in such conditions. But then one of my reasons for using the umbrella is that the wind is not strong, and so again my reasons do not apply. Finally, I may protest that opening my umbrella is my personal decision, and others can make their own decision as they see fit. They certainly can, but the fact remains that I am committed to the rationality of umbrella use under the specific conditions that induce me to open the umbrella. It would be as though I calculate that $7 + 8 = 15$ but insist that others can take the sum to be anything they want. They certainly can, but I am committed to the proposition that a sum of 15 is the rational conclusion. In the ethics realm, I might deduce that killing the innocent is wrong but insist that others can disagree if they want. They can disagree, but I have decided that they would be mistaken.

This whole analysis may appear to misunderstand human behavior, because we normally do not deliberate about our actions. When the rain starts, we open the umbrella without consciously considering the reasons for doing so, and similarly with countless everyday behaviors. This is certainly so, as human beings are creatures of habit and custom, and we often make decisions without conscious thought. Psychologists elaborate on this point by distinguishing "System 1" and "System 2" thinking in dual process theory, where the former is fast and unconscious, and the latter is slow and based on conscious reasoning (Kahneman, 2011). Ethicists have acknowledged the importance of habit and unconscious decision making at least since Aristotle. Yet we cultivate or learn habits at some point, and we allow them to continue. One may smoke cigarettes by habit, but there is an underlying decision not to break the habit. One may have learned to associate a person's outward appearance with behavioral characteristics, but one can decide to scrutinize such automatic judgments and correct them as necessary. These are the decisions that must be taken deliberately and evaluated ethically.

One reason that business constantly presents ethical challenges is that so many decisions must be taken consciously and deliberately. One cannot rely on unthinking habit when deciding whom to hire and lay off, whether to enter into a contract, how to set prices, when to close a plant, and so forth with a thousand other dilemmas. Reasons must be consciously adduced for each of these decisions, and those reasons subjected to ethical tests.

Ethical decision making in business therefore imposes a substantial burden. It is hard to bear this burden successfully without an intellectual framework within which to arrive at conclusions and generate consensus around them. The principles to follow provide such a framework.

3   Ethical principles

The generalization principle

The *generalization principle* says that I must generalize my action choices to everyone who shares my reasons, and be consistent in doing so. The principle follows directly from the two assumptions outlined in Chapter 2. If I choose an action, then I have a rationale for choosing it. Furthermore, the universality of reason says that I am choosing the action for everyone to whom my rationale applies. I must therefore believe that it is possible for me to act on my reasons while everyone else does the same. Otherwise my rationale is inconsistent and unintelligible.

An example may help explain this. Suppose I am walking through a store and decide to shoplift a pair of expensive headphones. I do so for two reasons: I would like to have new headphones, and the store has lax security. In reality, there may be other reasons as well, such as the fact that the store is insured for theft and no one will be directly harmed. But to simplify the argument, I will suppose I have only these two reasons. Due to the universality of reason, I must say that anyone in the store who would like to have new headphones should steal a pair. Yet I also know that many customers would, in fact, like to have new headphones. If they acted on my reasons, the headphones would quickly vanish from the shelf. The store would be forced to crack down with tighter security, spoiling my plans to get away with theft. So I am caught in a contradiction: I am deciding that anyone with my reasons to steal should do so, while at the same time I am *not* deciding that anyone with my reasons should do so, because I know that would defeat my own rationale for stealing.

The root problem here is that at least one of my reasons for stealing (lax security) is inconsistent with the assumption that others steal for the same reasons. This is a violation of the generalization principle, which may be stated:

> *Generalization principle: An action is ethical only if the agent can be rational in believing that the reasons for the action are consistent with the assumption that all others to whom the reasons apply perform the same action.*[1]

When applying this principle, it is important to state one's rationale in its full generality. For example, I might claim that I am stealing the headphones only because I want to listen to a recording of Maurice Ravel's *Daphnis and Chloé* in high fidelity. Security would still be lax if everyone who wants to hear this recording (i.e., practically no one) were to steal headphones. This shows that the rationale is generalizable, but it is not truly my rationale, because its scope is too narrow. The *scope* of a rationale is the set of possible circumstances I take to be sufficient to justify the action. Suppose I were eager to hear some piece of music other than *Daphnis and Chloé*. Would this alter my decision to steal? Of course not. The real reason I want the headphones is to hear music I really like, and a rationale with this broader scope is not generalizable. There are many customers who would fancy hearing music they really like on new headphones, and if they all pilfered headphones, security would tighten.

I might insist that I would never take the risk of shoplifting headphones for any other purpose than hearing my beloved *Daphnis and Chloé*. This is a bit reminiscent of a dieter who insists that he is munching high-calorie party snacks only because it is a special occasion. Yet what I would be inclined to do psychologically is not relevant. Rather, the problem is logical: I have no *rationale* for stealing in one case but not the other.

This entire discussion may seem to miss the point. Shoplifting head-phones is wrong because it is theft, not because the reasons behind it

---

[1]   This resembles Kant's (1785) famous Categorical Imperative we learn about in ethics courses, but it is by no means the same. Kant gives three "formula-tions" of the Imperative that are notoriously difficult to interpret precisely. One can find a modern interpretation in O'Neill's (2014) reconstruction of Kantian ethics.

lack certain logical niceties. Yet why is theft wrong? One might say it is wrong because it is illegal. But suppose the legislature never got around to passing a law against theft. Would that make it ethical? Actually, theft is normally wrong regardless of its legal status—because it is not generalizable. The argument goes like this. The concept of theft presupposes an institution of property. I steal something in order to keep it; that is, to make it my property. If people were to take things whenever they want, there would be no property. When I take merchandise from a store, others will feel free to take it from me minutes later. So taking things whenever we want, in order to possess and use them, is not generalizable because it undermines the social institution that makes possession and use possible.

The generalization principle yields several other rules of conduct that help make society and commerce possible. For example, breaking a promise merely for convenience is not generalizable, because if this were universal practice, it would be impossible to make meaningful promises in the first place. No one would take them seriously. In a similar vein, breaching an agreement or contract (which is a mutual promise) merely for convenience or profit is not generalizable. If it were universal practice, the social institution of agreements and contracts would break down. No one would enter into contracts, because they know the other parties will simply ignore them whenever they want. In fact, the whole point of engaging in a contract is that the parties honor it when they would rather not.

As a teacher, I cannot resist pointing out that cheating on an exam likewise fails generalizability. A common pair of reasons for cheating is that one can get away with it, and the resulting high grade will help one obtain a better job. Yet if cheating for these reasons were universal, the school would heavily proctor exams, so that students could no longer get away with cheating, or else employers would lose interest in grades because everyone makes an A and the grades have little meaning. In either case, one of the reasons for cheating is defeated. Similar arguments show that cheating in other areas of life usually lack generalizability, whether it be cheating on income tax or rigging a sports contest.

Perhaps the best-known feature of the generalization principle is its dim view of lying. A practice of lying when it is convenient to do so is not generalizable, at least when the lies must be believed to achieve their purpose. The obvious reason is that no one would, in fact, believe the lies, and they would not serve their purpose. This is not a blanket condemnation of all lying; as always, it depends on one's reasons. Skeptics of rational ethics predictably bring up the example of Anne Frank and her family, who hid from the Nazis in an Amsterdam office building during the 1940s.[2] Employees in the building lied to state police when they came knocking at the door, telling them that they had no idea where the Franks were hiding. The skeptics complain that rigid morality condemns lying in this case and, more broadly, cannot anticipate complicated real-life situations. Yet the lie was perfectly generalizable because of its rationale, which was to conceal the Franks' whereabouts from the police. If everyone falsely told the police they had no idea where fugitives from the Nazi regime were hiding, the police probably would not believe the lies, but they would be equally in the dark as to the fugitives' locations. The lies would still serve their purpose, perhaps even more effectively.

The generalization principle is therefore not "rigid" but can be quite subtle in application, because it takes into account the reasons for an action. While it can yield general rules against theft, promise breaking, cheating, or lying for mere convenience, it can also check whether these activities are wrong in specific situations where the reasons are more complicated than mere convenience.

The general rules also illustrate two useful rules of thumb for applying the generalization principle: an action fails the principle when its universal practice would *defeat the purpose of the action*, or when its universal practice would *undermine the social customs or institutions that make the action possible*. Generalized lying or cheating defeats the purpose of lying or cheating, while generalized theft or breach of promises undermines social practices that make property and promises possible.

We can wrap up this discussion of generalizability by defending a claim from Chapter 1: one cannot promise to do something unethical. The reason for this is that one can promise only to do what one can freely choose to do. An unethical "action" is not freely chosen due to the inco-

---

[2] As told in Frank (1947). A similar dilemma was raised in Kant's day by one of his critics, Benjamin Constant. Kant responded with an article (1797) that reflected his negative view of lying, although a hardline prohibition of all lying is not obviously implied by his writings (Sussman, 2009; Varden, 2010).

herence of its rationale; it is mere behavior. One cannot promise to steal any more than one can promise to hiccup.

The utilitarian principle

The *utilitarian principle* asks us to choose actions that most benefit those affected by our choices, while conforming to other ethical principles. The name derives from Jeremy Bentham's historical principle of utility (1780), which holds that the preferred action is the one that results in the greatest total utility. *Utility* is the ultimate end of our actions, which Bentham variously defined as happiness or pleasure.

Suppose, for example, that I am staying in a hotel and turn up the volume of my television at 2 am, to the point that other guests cannot sleep. I do so because the loud television helps me get my mind off my worries. This seems obviously unethical, but on what grounds? If there is a hotel rule against disturbing other guests, then one might argue that I agreed to abide by hotel rules when I checked in, and violating this agreement is not generalizable. Yet when other guests complain to the desk clerk about the noise, they are told that the hotel has no such rule and is not responsible for noisy guests. The disturbance seems nonetheless unethical, and we need a reason. The utilitarian principle fills this need. While the noise creates positive utility for me, it creates a great deal of negative utility for the other guests. My thoughtlessness reduces total net utility and is therefore unethical.

A major attraction of utilitarianism during the Enlightenment era was that it provided an objective, even scientific, way to judge actions ethically. Even when the consequences of an action choice cannot be predicted with certainty, one can use net expected utility as a criterion. It is computed by taking a weighted sum of the utilities that result from several possible outcomes of an action choice, where the weights are the probability of each outcome (see the Appendix for details).

A problem with the utilitarian principle, however, is showing that it is true. John Stuart Mill, another famous utilitarian, defended it with his observation that all people ultimately desire happiness or pleasure, because everything else they desire is a means to happiness or pleasure. He inferred from this that happiness is good and should be maximized (Mill, 1863). Aside from its questionable psychology, this is a rather obvious instance of the naturalistic fallacy. The mere fact that people universally desire something does not show it is good. Mill himself acknowledged, in a splendid example of understatement, that "ultimate ends are not amenable to direct proof" (Mill, 1863, p. 207). It is also unclear why the sum of individual utilities should be maximized without taking into account how they are distributed.

Fortunately, a utilitarian principle can be derived within the framework we are using here. Rather than view it as a *consequentialist* principle, as in the classical literature, we can view it the same way we view generalizability: as a *deontological* principle. Bentham's consequentialist principle judges an action solely by its utilitarian consequences. The principles we use are deontological (from the Greek for what is necessary or required) because they focus on what is required for the possibility of free action.

The first step in the deontological argument for utilitarianism is to explore more deeply the implications of our basic assumption that every action has a rationale. If someone asks why I rise early in the morning, I respond that I must do so to arrive at work on time. This is a rationale of sorts, but an incomplete one. Why arrive at work on time? It allows me to keep my job. So what? Well, keeping my job allows me to earn a living, and earning a living allows me to afford food and shelter, and food and shelter allow me to…what? To avoid an infinite regress of explanations that are never complete, there must at some point be a final goal that I regard as worthy for its own sake. There must be an end to which everything else is a means, or perhaps several ends. Let's say that happiness is one of the ends I ultimately seek.

The next step is to apply the universality of reason. Since I regard happiness as a worthy ultimate goal for me because it is *intrinsically* valuable, I must regard it as a worthy goal for anyone. I must therefore be rational in believing that my efforts to achieve happiness are consistent with others acting to achieve the same goal. Naturally, it is impossible for everyone to achieve maximum individual happiness; there must be compromises. Still, I must select an action that takes everyone's goal of achieving happiness as seriously as I take my own goal of achieving happiness.

It is hard to draw more specific conclusions from this argument. It does not seem to require strict maximization of total utility, nor does it require an equal distribution of utility. Suppose, for example, that a major storm strikes, and a power company must restore power to a large area as quickly as possible. It could restore power in urban areas first to maximize total utility, because power can be restored in more households more quickly in a densely populated area. However, this would result in extended blackouts for rural customers, perhaps even weeks or months.[3] On the other hand, if the power company attempted to equalize downtime for all customers, it would force long delays on thousands of urban customers while crews roam the countryside to serve a few rural customers just as quickly. The point is not that both extremes seem intuitively wrong, because we do not argue from intuitions. Rather, there is no apparent reason why either extreme is implied by the necessity of taking every customer's utility seriously. The power company is obligated to find some reasonable compromise between equity and efficiency while aiming for both. For example, restoring power in wealthy neighborhoods first is wrong, because it serves neither equity nor efficiency.

An important feature of the utilitarian principle is that it does not require one to consider unethical options when creating utility. This is for the same reason that one cannot promise something unethical: unethical options are not freely chosen actions. We can therefore answer the question, "Does the end justify the means?" In the context of the utilitarian principle, the end does not justify an *unethical* means, where the ethical status of the means is judged by the generalization and autonomy principles. By incorporating this proviso, we can state a utilitarian principle as follows:

Utilitarian principle: An act is ethical only if the agent can rationally believe that no available action both satisfies other ethical principles and would more effectively create utility for those affected by the choice of action.

In most practical business contexts, the effective creation of utility can be equated, in the classical fashion, with maximizing the sum of utilities over all affected. Utility can, in turn, normally be identified with such measur-

---

[3]   This, in fact, occurred in the aftermath of Hurricane Maria in Puerto Rico, the worst natural disaster to hit the island in recorded history.

able benefits as wealth or physical well-being. Even when measurements are not possible, common sense often suffices. There is no need for scientific quantification of happiness to conclude that my television should not disturb hotel guests.

The classical principle of utility is egalitarian to a certain degree, because everyone's utility counts equally, regardless of social station. Yet the distribution of utility becomes an important issue in some situations, as in the power restoration problem. There is no clear consensus on how equity and efficiency should be balanced in such cases, although *proportional fairness* has become a fairly standard approach in engineering. It is equivalent to the *Nash bargaining solution*, proposed by game theorist John Nash (1950), whose axiomatic argument gives it some degree of rational support. Proportional fairness is used, for example, to allocate bandwidth in telecommunications so as to increase throughput while not overly delaying any stream of packets, or to regulate traffic signal timing in a similar way. Other schemes for balancing equity and efficiency include alpha fairness (which generalizes proportional fairness), the Kalai–Smorodinsky bargaining solution, and methods for combining a Rawlsian maximin criterion with utility maximization. These are discussed in the Appendix.

The clause about rational belief in the utilitarian principle acknowledges that the outcome of an action choice is often hard to predict. We need only make sure that, to the best of our knowledge and evidence, no alternative action would be more effective at delivering utility. This does not give us license to be lazy, however. For example, company managers who introduce a new food additive cannot simply say that, as far they know, the additive is safe. They must research the matter until its safety is established. This is an area where ethics and rational self-interest are similar. It would be irrational for me to invest in a piece of real estate I have never seen, simply because I am not aware of any problems with it. I should obviously check out the property. When making decisions that affect others, I should be as prudent as I would be if my own interests were at stake, and even more prudent when my choice affects many others. On the other hand, it is irrational to invest time in researching small decisions that have little impact.

The main implication of utilitarianism for business is that its activities should be beneficial. Fortunately, commerce and trade tend to increase overall utility, by their very nature. Buyers and sellers generally enter into a transaction only when both benefit. Customers purchase merchandise only when it is worth more to them than the price paid; the difference is "consumer surplus," in the language of economics. It is the same, in reverse, for sellers, who benefit from "producer surplus." This increase in utility is, again, only a general tendency of commerce. An ethical business must take care that its particular products and activities genuinely enhance utility. This obligation is discussed further in Chapter 5.

The autonomy principle

The *autonomy principle* tells us not to coerce others, or otherwise interfere with the ethical actions of others, without informed or implied consent. It tends to resonate more strongly with individualistic cultures than the utilitarian principle, but it is easily misunderstood. It does not say, for example, that I can do anything I want as long as I do not interfere with the actions of others.

To make the autonomy principle precise, we must speak of *action plans* rather than simply actions. An action plan has the form, "If such-and-such reasons apply, then I will do such-and-such." Since every action is accompanied by a set of reasons that are taken to justify the action, every action is an action plan. Suppose, for example, that I decide to cross the street to a bus stop, because I want to catch a bus, and no traffic is coming. My action plan is, "If I want to catch a bus as soon as possible, and there is a bus stop across the street, and no traffic is coming, then I will cross the street now." If you grab my arm and prevent me from walking into oncoming traffic, there is no coercion because your action plan is consistent with mine. I never intended to cross the street when traffic is coming. However, if you grab me when there is no traffic, this is coercive and violates the autonomy principle, which we can state as follows:

Autonomy principle: An action plan is unethical if the agent is rationally constrained to believe it interferes with the ethical action plans of some collection of other agents without informed or implied consent.

This requires some unpacking. First, one is "rationally constrained" to believe that there is interference when it would be irrational not to believe so. Suppose, for example, that a construction crew leaves a deep manhole uncovered and unprotected, whereupon someone falls in and suffers serious injury. While serious injury interferes with many action plans, the crew is not rationally constrained to believe that an accident will, in fact, occur. They violate the utilitarian principle, since an accident is more or less probable, but not the autonomy principle. On the other hand, if the open and unmarked manhole is in a London pavement jammed with pedestrians, the crew violates autonomy, because they are rationally constrained to believe that an accident is inevitable. They do not know who will suffer injury, but their action plan is inconsistent with the action plans of a *collection* of agents, namely London pedestrians.

The autonomy principle allows coercion when there is informed and/or implied consent. Suppose I attend a concert at which there is an announcement that photography is strictly prohibited, and violators will be removed from the hall. Nonetheless I hold up my smart phone to record the concert, and the ushers compel me to leave. This is coercion, but by recording the performers, I gave implied consent to be removed. In effect, my action plan was, "If I wish to record the performance, and I am not caught and removed from the hall, then I will record the performance." The ushers did not interfere with this plan.

The autonomy principle also allows interference with unethical behavior, because unethical "actions" are not autonomous, and so there is no violation of autonomy. I can exercise self-defense against someone who wants to attack me, because attacks are unethical. I can stand between a bicycle and a would-be thief, because theft is unethical. I can erect "no trespassing" signs and a fence on my property to keep people out, even though this interferes with their plan to walk harmlessly across my land. This is because, at least in my legal jurisdiction, it is illegal and therefore unethical to trespass when permission to do so is denied, and the sign constitutes denial. On the other hand, I cannot lock my employees in a closet to prevent them from submitting false expense reports, because this interferes with many perfectly ethical action plans.[4]

---

[4]   See Chapter 6 of Hooker (2018) for a fuller discussion of when coercion is permissible to prevent unethical behavior.

The autonomy principle does not say I can do anything I want as long as I do not interfere with the actions of others. It and the other principles we derive are only necessary, and not sufficient, conditions for ethical behavior. It is possible to violate the generalization or utilitarian principle while interfering with no one's action plans, and doing so is unethical.

In my experience, the most widespread misunderstanding of autonomy is to suppose that depriving people of what they want violates their autonomy. Suppose that a certain shop is the only cigarette vendor in town and decides to end sales of cigarettes, on the ground that they are unhealthy. Customers complain that this paternalistic action violates their "right" or "freedom" to buy what they want. Yet it is no violation of autonomy, because it interferes with no action plan. Customers cannot have an action plan of being sold cigarettes, because this is an action taken by the store owners, not the customer. Customers can only decide to buy cigarettes if they are for sale. A refusal to sell cigarettes does not interfere with this action plan. In general, an action plan can only specify what the agent, and not someone else, is going to do.

On the other hand, a prison guard who refuses to provide inmates with food and water violates autonomy. While the prisoners cannot have an action plan of being provided food and water, because this is not something they decide, they have many other ethical action plans that cannot be carried out if there is no food or water. Deprivation of necessities interferes with these action plans and therefore violates autonomy.

Two case studies revisited

The two case studies introduced in Chapter 1 provide an opportunity to see ethical principles in action. In fact, the full meaning and implications of these principles cannot be appreciated until they are applied to real dilemmas. One must study a number of applications to build the skills necessary to resolve dilemmas, just as a mathematics student must work through many proofs to learn how to demonstrate new theorems.

In the Ford Pinto case, the company decided not to recall cars with defective fuel tanks because the costs of doing so outweighed the benefits. This was a legitimate utilitarian calculation, because everyone affected by the decision was taken into account, including those victimized by exploding cars. The decision could therefore plausibly be seen as passing the utilitarian test, at least in its classical formulation as utility maximization. Ford's mistake was to assume that this is the only ethical principle it must observe.

In fact, Ford's decision violated the autonomy principle. Its managers were rationally constrained to believe that a failure to fix the defect would lead to serious injury and death. In fact, this had already occurred. Since serious injury and death interfere with many ethical action plans, this is a violation of autonomy.

One may ask, however, whether customers had given informed or implied consent to the risk of driving a Pinto. Every auto manufacturer knows that people will be seriously injured and killed in the cars they sell. They can argue that anyone who rides in a car knows that a serious accident is possible. Customers therefore give informed consent to the risk, and manufacturers can sell cars without violation of autonomy. Yet there was something different about the Ford Pinto. It had a defect that posed exceptional danger known only to the manufacturer. Drivers and passengers did not voluntarily assume this kind of risk, because they were unaware of it. Rather, they assumed the level of risk of a typical car. Since there was no informed consent, Ford's decision not to recall was a clear violation of the autonomy principle and therefore unethical.

This argument does not show, however, that Ford must pay the $11 cost of correcting the defect in a recalled car. It could alert owners as in a normal recall and urge them to bring the car to a Ford dealer to be fixed at their own expense. Customers who declined to do so would knowingly assume the risk of driving the car, and Ford would supposedly be off the hook. Yet at this point we can turn to the generalization principle, which imposes a general obligation to honor one's contracts. The defective fuel tank was probably covered by a written warranty that was part of the sales contract and therefore binding on the dealer or the manufacturer. The customer should therefore not have to pay the $11.

Even if the written warranty was unclear or non-existent, one can argue that the Pinto's defect was covered by an implied warranty, in particular a *warranty of merchantability*. This is based on the idea that there is an implicit promise in any sale, namely that the product is fit for the purpose for which it is sold. If I sell you a can of beans, I promise that there are edible beans inside the can. However, if I sell you a chain saw that could fly apart and slice up your face, this product is not fit for its purpose and violates a warranty of merchantability. A car is used for many purposes, such as driving one's kids to school. Since a low-speed collision in the school parking lot could incinerate the kids, one may argue that a defective Ford Pinto was no more fit for its purpose than the defective chain saw is for cutting wood. If so, Ford was obligated to pay the $11 even if there was no express warranty.[1]

---

[1]   A manufacturer may also be legally liable for damages if there is negligence or lack of due care, with the specifics depending on the jurisdiction. In the U.S., a manufacturer is held liable for damages due to a product defect, even if there is no negligence. This doctrine of *strict liability* is based on case law, not statute.

Guidant defibrillators

While the Ford Pinto case is straightforward, the Guidant defibrillator case is quite challenging. Like Ford, Guidant conducted a utilitarian analysis and obtained analogous results. It determined that a failure to notify doctors and patients of the defibrillator's defect was utilitarian, because it resulted in less lethal risk for patients. Although the utility-maximizing choice was not the ethical one for Ford, it was arguably the right choice for Guidant.

One might object to the utilitarian choice based on a strong intuition that patients have a right to know about a defective implant so that they can choose what to do about it. Since Guidant kept them in the dark, it allegedly violated their autonomy. Yet, as always, right claims do not prove anything; they are only claims. An argument is needed. One might begin with an observation that patients *want* to know about their health status, which we can grant. Yet the autonomy principle does not require Guidant to give patients anything they want, simply because they want it. There was no violation of autonomy because there was no interference with patient action plans. Patients may have wanted to be informed about defects, but they could not have an action plan of being informed, because this was Guidant's decision, not theirs. They could only have an action plan specifying what they would do if informed, and Guidant did not interfere with this plan. This is a case where moral intuitions, even strongly held ones, are misleading.

One might take another tack by arguing that Guidant's silence violated autonomy because it inevitably resulted in the deaths of some patients due to device failure. Yet we must ask whether a decision to remain silent actually interfered with the action plans of Guidant's customers. The situation here is different than for Ford. Ford's decision not to recall defective Pintos interfered with action plans by increasing the risk of injury or death for its customers. Guidant's decision to leave defibrillators in place did not increase the risk to its customers. On the contrary, it reduced their risk. So it is difficult to say that Guidant's decision interfered with their plans.

The outcome could be different if the facts of the case were somewhat different. Suppose, for example, that Guidant had strong evidence that the risk of replacement was actually lower than the risk of failure for a subgroup of patients, perhaps young patients like Joshua. Then there was a collection of agents (young patients) whose autonomy was violated by Guidant's decision, because Guidant knew that leaving the defibrillators in place would increase their risk. The company would have been obligated to inform them and their doctors of the defect. This action may not maximize utility, because some older patients would probably get word of the defect and demand a replacement, exposing themselves to unnecessary risk. Yet it satisfies the utilitarian principle, because no available option creates greater expected utility while respecting patient autonomy. It also satisfies the autonomy principle, because older patients who request a replacement give informed consent to the additional risk. In any event, the case description of Sandbu and Wen (2008) does not indicate that Guidant had risk data for specific patient subgroups, and we proceed on this assumption.

It remains to consider the generalization test. As in the Pinto case, the warranty is not a central issue, because warranties do not generally impose an obligation to notify the customer of defects. Guidant may have been obligated to supply a cost-free replacement on request, depending on how the manufacturer's warranty was written.[2] Such an obligation would not obviously derive from a warranty of merchantability, however, since the defibrillator was fit for its purpose despite a small chance of malfunction. The defective units represented the state of the art at the time they were implanted and doubtless saved many lives. Patients clearly would not have regarded them as unfit for their purpose if they had known about the risk of failure, because they were willing to install a new one at significantly greater risk.

A more serious generalizability issue is whether Guidant's failure to notify patients was *deceptive*. By its silence, the company may have misled patients into believing that no defect had been discovered. Guidant never lied to patients, but one can deceive without lying. Deception is *causing someone to believe something you know is false*. Suppose, for example, that I undergo a series of medical tests with good results except for a spot on the chest X-ray. It is lung cancer. The doctor sends me a copy of the test

---

2   A U.S. manufacturer may also be subject to strict liability for defective medical devices, although they present more complicated legal issues than non-medical products.

results but omits the X-ray report. The doctor is not lying to me, because all the reports I receive are true, but she is deceiving me by causing me to believe I am in good health. In the same sense, Guidant may have caused patients to have the false belief that there was no known defect in their defibrillators. Yet it was not part of Guidant's purpose to cause anyone to have any particular belief. It was enough that patients *not have* a belief that their device required replacement. In fact, the true scope of Guidant's rationale was simply to reduce the risk to their customers. To run the generalization test on this rationale, we can suppose that it is universal practice not to inform patients of defects when doing so would increase patient risk. Then it seems rational to believe that Guidant would still be able to reduce risk by failing to inform patients of defects. In fact, such a practice may already be largely generalized, given that the government expressly allowed it.

Guidant's decision therefore appears to pass all the ethical tests, although somewhat more specific risk data could have called for a different action. Unfortunately, the decision failed to achieve its objective in the end, because the news media publicized the defect. If Guidant could have rationally anticipated this, or even given it some probability, the utilitarian calculation could have been different. To make things worse, the financial incentives created by an imminent buyout strengthened the public perception that the company was acting purely in self-interest, without regard to patient welfare.

Ethical choices can be hard, both in formation and execution, even when there is a rational basis for the choices. But without a rational basis, the ethical path is not only hard but uncharted as well.

5 Corporations

What is a corporation?

There is perhaps no more divisive topic in business than the role and influence of corporations. It goes beyond the scope of this book to ask whether corporations should exist and what form they should take. These are public policy questions requiring concepts and tools not developed here. Yet we can address the ethical duties incurred by corporations in their current form, as well as ethical dilemmas that managers, employees, and shareholders encounter in a corporate environment. A necessary first step is to understand what exactly a corporation is, and what purpose it serves.

Corporations result from the confluence of three historical developments: joint stock ownership, government charters, and limited liability. *Joint stock ownership* allows multiple investors to pool their assets and receive returns based on their stake in the company. The idea has precursors in seventh-century China and developed gradually in Europe during the sixteenth century. Joint ownership not only provides a mechanism for accumulating private capital, but it can also allow a company to outlive any of its owners and thereby achieve long-term stability. Joint stock companies with government *charters* also began to appear in Europe during the sixteenth century. While frequently a means to grant monopolies to organizations favored by the crown, the charter also allowed governments to regulate commerce by specifying the conditions under which major economic players could operate.

The famous Dutch East India Company (VOC), chartered in 1602, was the first company with permanent capital stock that could be bought and sold by the public. It established the world's first stock exchange in Amsterdam for this purpose. Even at this early time, Dutch companies frequently offered *limited liability* to non-managing investors, meaning that they could lose their investment if the company failed but were not otherwise responsible for its debts. The VOC extended this protection to managing directors and is often regarded as the prototype of the modern business corporation. Limited liability was not established by law until 1811 in New York state and 1855 in England, but it is a regular feature of corporate legal systems today.

A number of variations on the standard business corporation have evolved, with the details differing widely across jurisdictions. They include *non-stock* corporations, which have members rather than shareholders, as well as *not-for-profit* corporations, which are always non-stock. *Privately held* corporations have shareholders but do not trade stock publicly, and they are consequently subject to fewer reporting requirements. Many privately held companies are not chartered as corporations but provide corporate-style limited liability to owners. Examples include the *Gesellschaft mit beschränkter Haftung* (GmbH) in Germany, the private limited company (Ltd) in the United Kingdom, and the limited liability company (LLC) in the U.S., the last of which is basically a partnership with limited-liability protection.

Despite the plethora of corporate forms, one can see the fundamental purpose of a business corporation to be raising private capital under some degree of public oversight. Limited-liability provisions make it easier to attract investors by reducing their risk. Corporations therefore play a vital role in capital accumulation and creation of wealth, with at least the potential for public regulation. While we tend to associate the corporate world with such behemoths as BP, Amazon, and Siemens, many corporations are small and provide a useful tool for ordinary business people. At least in the U.S., an individual can obtain a corporate charter for a very modest fee and without legal counsel. On the other hand, the twin advantages of private capital accumulation and economy of scale allow transnational corporations to achieve enormous size and influence, often enabling them to circumvent regulation by national governments. Their often single-minded focus on maximizing shareholder value can lead to the neglect of other values, such as employee and customer well-being and environmental sustainability. We examine some of these issues in this and subsequent chapters.

Corporate governance

A major consequence of joint stock ownership is a separation between owners on the one hand and managers and employees on the other, except in cases in which managers or employees are themselves the primary owners. One must therefore ask what obligations managers and employees have to the owners. The most obvious is fiduciary duty, which derives from an agency agreement with the owners. While it was noted in Chapter 1 that fiduciary duty is not the basis of business ethics, as often supposed, it is nonetheless a duty. An almost universal structural mechanism for carrying out this duty is to assign it to a *board of directors*.

The composition of corporate boards reflects the larger culture in which they operate. In the Anglo-American sphere, directors are typically elected by stockholders, whose voting power is proportional to their shareholdings. Stockholders also vote on major company decisions at an annual meeting. In practice, stockholders often fill out a proxy card that allows a top manager or other person to vote on their behalf, perhaps according to instructions on the card. The board of directors selects a CEO and perhaps other officers, although it is not unusual for the CEO to serve as board chair. The latter practice is often seen as less than ideal, because board members are tasked with overseeing management on behalf of owners. The Anglo-American corporate board affords employees practically no influence in running the firm, and the board and management team must therefore take care to carry out ethical obligations that the owners have to employees as well as other stakeholders.

In continental Europe, the board often consists of two tiers: a supervisory board and a non-overlapping management board. The supervisory board oversees general company strategy and performance and selects professional managers to form the executive board. Because the firm tends to rely largely on debt financing, rather than equity financing obtained from stock sales, supervisory boards typically reflect the interests of banks and other financiers. The board may be legally required to include employee representatives, as for example in Germany and Sweden, so that employees typically have greater influence than in the Anglo-American model.

Corporate government in Asia follows several models, in which personal relationships often play a key role. Chinese law requires that companies have a board of directors and a board of supervisors, where the former determines company policy and the latter oversees the performance and conduct of the directors. In practice, the company is often controlled by a wealthy individual or family, or by the government. Japanese firms tend to have a single, rather large governing board, many of whose members have relationships with banks and other firms. The firm is often part of a horizontal *keiretsu*, which is an alliance of several companies and a bank that finances them, and perhaps a vertical *keiretsu*, which links a firm with its suppliers and helps to enable the famous just-in-time inventory management practices pioneered by the Japanese. These relationships impose cultural obligations that have a major influence over the operation of the firm.

The prevailing structure of corporate governance implies that governing board members, and not employees at large, are bound by fiduciary duty to owners and investors. This duty generally extends to executives, because they are hired to operate the firm on behalf of the board. While lower-ranking employees might be told they should engage in some (perhaps questionable) activity because of their fiduciary duty to maximize profit for the firm, this is incorrect, because they do not enter into the agency agreement that imposes fiduciary duty. Rather, employees enter into a contractual arrangement with the firm, which generally implies an obligation to abide by company rules and directives that are related to the conduct of business, so long as these rules and directives are ethical. An employee might very well be obligated to act against the interests of owners if directed to do so by company management. As for members of the governing board, their obligations are discussed in Chapter 1: because they act as agents for owners and other investors, they are required to serve the financial interests of their principals only by means of actions that would be ethical for the principals themselves to undertake.

The legal interpretation of fiduciary duty is normally limited to the financial interests of owners and investors. Typically, company directors are not legally required to reflect the desires of their principals in other matters, such as the content of advertising or choice of products to bring to market. This is to discourage owners from meddling in company management, and to protect directors from frivolous lawsuits. Even with respect to financial management, courts normally do not attempt to second guess whether directors make the right business decisions. It is enough that they make a good faith effort, and lawsuits against directors are usually based on conflicts of interest, negligence, illegal activities, or self-dealing. Nonetheless, if there is concern that directors will suffer lawsuits for sacrificing maximum profit in the pursuit of ethical goals, incorporation as a *benefit corporation* offers one means of legal protection. This type of charter, available in 35 American states, recognizes such non-financial goals as positive impact on society. A benefit corporation should be distinguished from a *B-corp*, which has no legal status but is a company certified to have met particular social and environmental criteria. B-corp certification is available internationally from a non-profit organization known as B Lab.

In general, corporate governance structures are not suitable for stockholder-directed management, except perhaps for a few general policies ratified at annual stockholder meetings. This is due in part to the widespread use of proxies and a dearth of forums for debate and consensus building. Nonetheless, activist shareholders can sometimes exert influence over specific company policies, perhaps through resolutions presented at annual shareholder meetings, publicity campaigns, proxy battles, or takeover threats. Another possible avenue for shareholder influence is socially responsible investing (SRI), discussed below.

Corporate social responsibility

The role of corporations as the major source of private capital accumulation, and their resulting influence on world affairs, demand an assessment of their responsibility to society. Corporate social responsibility (CSR) can be broadly understood as imposing three types of obligations:

- A corporation's products should benefit the customers who buy them.
- The products should benefit the larger society while causing no significant harm to the natural environment.
- Company activities other than the creation of goods and services should likewise have a beneficial effect.

These obligations are primarily utilitarian in nature, but generalizability and autonomy frequently play a role as well. We consider each type of obligation in turn.

Obligations to customers

The utilitarian obligation to customers may seem obvious, but it has been disputed. Many see no ethical problem with selling potentially harmful products, such as cigarettes or unhealthy fast food, provided the purchasers are adults and fully informed of the risks. Since consumers buy the product voluntarily, it is said, the company should not be held "responsible" for the consequences of their free choices. Yet such sales can conflict with the utilitarian principle, which is concerned only with the utility or disutility that ultimately results, regardless of whether it is mediated by the free choices of others. Suppose, for example, that a pharmaceutical company must choose between two possible new products: an anti-viral drug that will relieve massive suffering, and an anti-wrinkle cream. Although the two products are projected to be equally profitable, the utilitarian principle obliges the company to opt for the anti-viral drug. This is despite the fact that the benefits of the drug depend on the free choices of doctors to prescribe it and patients to use it. There is little reason to deny that the company is "responsible" for the enormous good it creates with this marketing decision.

Some argue that paternalistic marketing decisions violate the "right" or "freedom" of customers to buy what they want. Suppose that a certain shop is the only cigarette vendor in town and decides to end sales of cigarettes, on the ground that they are unhealthy. Customers may see this as restricting free choice, but it is no violation of autonomy, because it interferes with no action plan. Customers cannot have an action plan of being sold cigarettes, because this is an action taken by the store owners, not the customer. Customers can only decide to buy cigarettes if they are for sale. A refusal to sell cigarettes does not interfere with this action plan and therefore does not violate autonomy.

Obligations to society at large and the environment

Utilitarian duties to create generally beneficial products and services, which may again seem incontestable, have nonetheless been criticized. While perhaps granting that a company should not harm society or the environment, critics of utilitarianism point out that the principle demands more than this. It requires the company to *maximize* utility. This may seem to take all the fun and frivolity out of life, because selling balloons or candy bars creates less utility than selling life-saving antibiotics and is therefore presumably unethical. Yet ethics is not so puritanical. There is no utilitarian obligation to market products that create the greatest utility per unit sold, because doing so is not generalizable. If it were generalized, we would lack the many everyday items that are necessary for our existence and well-being (ranging from screwdrivers to toilet paper), and this would defeat the goal of maximizing overall utility. Selling balloons and candy is both generalizable and utilitarian in a developed economy, if the reasons for doing so include the fact that other producers are meeting basic needs. It may be disutilitarian, however, in a poor country where the necessities of life are in short supply.[1]

Other obligations

The third CSR category covers activities other than the creation of goods and services, which likewise have an enormous impact. They include employment, labor relations, advertising, pricing, investor relations, finance, natural resource consumption, and waste generation. These are discussed in later chapters, including a chapter devoted entirely to sustainability.

Finally, CSR is often associated with pro bono activities, such as investing in local infrastructure, funding social service activities, or patronizing the arts. Diverting company funds to these activities can certainly enhance net utility by improving quality of life, provided the firm is well enough established that the cost to its financial health does not outweigh the benefits. Yet the primary utilitarian contribution of business is achieved by doing what it does best: creating valuable products and services in a socially and environmentally responsible way.

---

[1] A long-standing objection to utilitarianism is that it is too demanding in general. Yet the mere fact that a principle seems too demanding does not show it is wrong. In any case, many of utilitarianism's harsh demands vanish when the generalization principle is applied, as in the discussion above. Responses to the "demandingness objection" include those of Singer (1972), Kagan (1989), Unger (1996), and Norcross (1997). Objections are revived in Murphy (2000) and Mulgan (2001), with a response from Sobel (2007). See Hooker (2018) for further arguments on this issue.

Socially responsible investing

A popular means for shareholders to influence corporate behavior is to invest in accordance with social principles. SRI has become increasingly popular since the 1960s, although it has much older roots, particularly in religious traditions. The eighteenth-century cleric John Wesley, one of the founders of Methodism, argued against investing in companies that subjected their employees to dangerous working conditions. Traditional Islamic teachings discourage investment in companies that rely excessively on interest income or participate in *haram* activities. The ethical investing movement received a major boost in the late 1970s and 1980s, when some universities (under student pressure) protested South African apartheid by divesting from firms doing business there. Hundreds of socially responsible mutual funds have since appeared, and SRI has become a global industry. This trend is reflected in socially and religiously oriented stock indices, such as the S&P 500 Environmentally and Socially Responsible Index, the Dow Jones Islamic Market Index, and the FTSE Global Equity Shariah Index Series.

The most obvious ethical basis for SRI is the utilitarian principle, since investor preferences for ethical companies could result in greater net utility creation. Yet it raises the basic empirical question as to whether SRI actually influences corporate behavior, or more relevantly for the principle, whether one can be rational in believing that it has no measurable effect. If the latter is true, the utilitarian principle imposes no obligation to invest in socially responsible companies. Classical economic theory supports this view, because textbook perfect-market assumptions imply that SRI has no effect on share price, and therefore presumably no effect on company behavior. This is essentially because other investors stand ready to buy shares that the socially responsible investor eschews. Yet the economics literature also recognizes market imperfections that could invalidate this conclusion (Rivoli, 2003). As for empirical evidence of an SRI impact, it is hard to find consensus in the literature, except perhaps on the need for more research (Hellsten and Mallin, 2006; Van Dijk-de Groot and Nijhof, 2015; Piper, 2018). On the other hand, recent research on the characteristics of socially responsible investors indicates a growing interest in how to attract this large group of investors (Chamorro-Mera, 2018; Signori, 2020). This suggests that they may be influencing business decisions.

Even if widespread ethical investing has an impact, this alone does not establish a utilitarian obligation on the individual investor. The utilitarian principle is concerned with the effect of an individual's action choice, not the effect of a widespread practice. This relieves small investors, at least, of a utilitarian obligation to invest in ethical companies. A small investor's actions have no discernible effect on corporate behavior; or at any rate, the investor is not rationally constrained to believe otherwise. This leads to a *futility argument*, which often surfaces in utilitarian discussions: if I don't do it, someone else will. More specifically, if I don't invest in an objectionable company, someone else will, and I therefore have no utilitarian obligation to invest ethically. The argument is, in fact, valid as far as the utilitarian principle is concerned, although other principles may be relevant. Prison guards who are ordered to torture a prisoner might also use a futility argument by pointing out that if they refuse, they will be replaced by others who will obey the command. Yet torturing prisoners is wrong because it violates autonomy, even if others are willing to carry out the torture in one's stead. It is unclear, however, how to defend an SRI obligation for the small investor based on principles other than utility.

It may seem paradoxical that the utilitarian principle would not encourage a small shareholder to invest in ethical firms when an overall trend of doing so increases utility. Yet this is simply because a small shareholder cannot influence company behavior. Ethics only requires people to do what they have the power to do ("ought implies can"). If a small investor can even slightly influence the probability that a company will mend its ways, perhaps through shareholder activism or speaking out, then there is a utilitarian obligation to do so—unless, of course, the time and effort would be better spent on some other ethical cause. The utilitarian principle may even require divestment if this would enhance the activist's influence, perhaps by avoiding a charge of hypocrisy. Yet a mere choice to invest in an unethical firm is consistent with the utilitarian principle, so long as there is no reason to believe the choice is in fact disutilitarian.

One must also consider the utilitarian effect on small investors themselves, since socially responsible portfolios may yield less return. The lion's share of SRI-related research deals with just this question. Widespread interest in this research may merely reflect a desire to feel good about oneself without actually making a sacrifice. Yet it is ethically relevant, because the utilitarian principle cares as much about one's own utility as another's. If contributions to an SRI fund reduce the small investor's return, when there is not a scintilla of evidence for a positive social effect, then those contributions are unethical. The utilitarian principle therefore directs small investors to focus on their own returns—unless, again, this would interfere with a utilitarian obligation to promote ethical corporate behavior through some other means.

In the meantime, a large fund might well have a utilitarian obligation to invest ethically, because its portfolio can have a material effect on company behavior. Its actions can also trigger a bandwagon effect that includes smaller investors, as occurred to some extent during the apartheid controversy. Large funds that are reluctant to divest in questionable companies, due to the lower returns that would result, may cite fiduciary responsibility as a reason for their hesitation. This defense is valid only if the investors themselves have no obligation to favor ethical companies. While this is true of smaller investors, as just argued, they would have such an obligation if they were in charge of the fund, and this is what matters. Thus when the massive Teachers Insurance and Annuity Association was called upon to divest from South Africa in the 1980s, they had an ethical obligation to do so, unless the resulting financial losses to their investors would have outweighed any positive influence on the situation in South Africa. The "unless" clause is not based on fiduciary duty, but simply on the fact that the utilitarian principle directs one to maximize utility.

Insider trading

Insider trading is usually defined as buying and selling stocks (or other securities) based on information that is not available to the public. Insider trades are normally executed by executives or board members who have access to privileged information. Various forms of this practice are illegal in most jurisdictions, although the level of enforcement varies widely, and the laws may be ignored completely.

Common objections to insider trading are that it is "unfair" to other investors, or does not provide them a "level playing field." These arguments are of little value for resolving the matter. Notions of fairness are notoriously vague and vary a great deal, depending on who cries "unfair." It is equally unclear why the metaphor of a playing field applies to stock trading. Players in a sporting contest voluntarily commit to an explicitly defined set of rules. Violating the rules of the game simply to win is indeed ungeneralizable, because if it were generalized, there would be no game to win. Yet stock trading is a "game" only in a figurative sense, because there is no agreed-upon rulebook as in football or cricket. One might argue that securities laws provide a rulebook, but we can grant that insider trading is unethical if it is illegal. This does not settle whether the practice is inherently unethical apart from legal constraints, nor whether it *should* be illegal.

A utilitarian defense of insider trading might begin with the observation that stock trading creates more value if investors are well informed about the companies in which they invest. This helps ensure that money is directed to firms that will succeed, thus presumably increasing overall utility. Executives who believe in their firm's potential, due to intimate knowledge of products under development, can perhaps boost expected utility by buying its stock. Executives who know that their firm is about to go under can sell their stock and invest the proceeds in companies that are more likely to create value.

While this general observation has merit, a utilitarian assessment must be specific to the situation. Dumping stocks may add to the firm's instability by deflating stock prices or undermining confidence among investors who learn of the sale. This could trigger a selloff that destroys the firm before it can manage its decline in an orderly fashion. The resulting loss in utility could easily offset any potential benefit of investing in a healthier firm. Whether it would do so is a question of fact that must be settled by knowledge of the specific situation.

Even if an insider's stock sale creates positive net utility, it may not be generalizable. A sale that incurs even a small risk of harming the firm is an instance of self-dealing and is arguably inconsistent with fiduciary duty. A breach of fiduciary duty in this situation is ungeneralizable because it violates the underlying agency agreement purely for personal gain.

An insider sale may be ungeneralizable on broader grounds as well. One must ask if the purposes of insider trading could be achieved if it were practiced by all who would benefit from it. One might argue that the stock market would attract fewer investors, an outcome that is perhaps inconsistent with the insider's goal of reaping personal benefit. This is, in fact, one way of spelling out the "level playing field" argument. Yet it is a hard case to make, because economists widely disagree on the effects of widespread insider trading, and in particular whether it would alienate investors. One might therefore rationally believe that insider trading is generalizable so long as it conforms to fiduciary duty.

In summary, insider trading is ethical only if it enhances net expected utility overall and would not be seen by investors as self-dealing that could potentially harm the firm. These conditions are normally met by a stock purchase based on an insider's anticipation of a bright future for the firm, but probably not by a selloff based on inside knowledge of an impending downturn.

Even when an act of insider trading is ethical apart from legal considerations, it may be unethical if prohibited by law. Violating the law merely for personal gain is almost always ungeneralizable, because if everyone did so, the resulting anarchy would likely be inconsistent with any sort of personal gain. The situation is different if insider trading laws on the books are universally ignored, and the possibility of personal gain remains nonetheless. In this case, insider trading is ethical if it is utility enhancing and consistent with fiduciary duty.

Worker ownership

A corporation is typically owned or financed by stockholders, bankers, or venture capitalists who do not work for the firm. The resulting separation of capital and labor has given rise to two centuries of ideological struggle over the merits and ills of capitalism. Yet nothing in the concept of a corporation requires this separation. Workers can incorporate their own company to form what is widely known as a *worker cooperative* (Vieta et al., 2016). They may own shares of stock in the corporation or simply serve as governing members of a jointly held company. They can designate professional managers or participate equally in management, the latter type of organization comprising a *worker collective*. In either case, the workers determine all aspects of company policy. Many worker cooperatives adopt principles promulgated by the International Cooperative

Alliance (2020), which was founded in 1895 and represents cooperative organizations in 109 countries.

The origin of worker cooperatives is usually traced to Robert Owen, who operated the New Lanark textile mill in Scotland on socialist principles beginning in 1800, and who attempted to set up cooperative communities in the United Kingdom, U.S., and Canada. The modern cooperative movement arose in the 1950s and accelerated in the 1960s. The largest and most famous cooperative enterprise is the Mondragon Corporation, founded in 1956 in the Basque region of Spain and today employing more than 80,000 people.

While discussion of worker cooperatives is often a battle between socialist and capitalist ideology, one can analyze them strictly from an ethical perspective. Issues of social organization are beyond the scope of this book, but we can ask whether there are ethical arguments for organizing one's business as a worker-owned enterprise. Cooperatives are frequently advocated on the ground that they are more democratic (Summers and Chillas, 2019), less prone to income inequality, more likely to balance profitability with the welfare of workers, more likely to succeed due to worker buyin, and more likely to preserve jobs in a market downturn by reducing wages rather than laying off workers. These arguments can be construed as based on principles of autonomy or utility.

An autonomy argument might be built on an observation that workplace democracy allows workers greater control over their lives. There are two difficulties with an argument of this sort, however. One is the practical issue of how to raise start-up capital without yielding to outside control. While there is no formal inconsistency in the idea of a worker-owned corporation, there is a fundamental tension. The primary function of a business corporation is raising private capital, and most workers cannot afford to contribute capital. They can be asked to dedicate part of their wages to purchasing company stock once it is started, but the company must get started. This implies that worker ownership is either inaccessible to most people or must rely on outside financing of some sort, such as bank loans. To ensure workplace democracy, the outside financiers must be willing to lend money without demanding a role in the firm's decision making (as is common in the debt-financed firms of continental Europe and Japan) or placing intrusive restrictions on how the firm is to be managed.

Even if the financial barriers can be overcome, autonomy arguments usually fail in this context. While traditionally financed corporations may permit workers less control over their lives, this lack of control generally does not rise to the level of autonomy violation. Workers who voluntarily sign on with a company give implied consent to typical business-related company directives that regulate much of their lives. This is not to say that management can do anything it wants because employees can always quit the company (a fallacy discussed in Chapter 6). But it does say that management can impose typical business policies on workers without violating their autonomy.

Even if greater control over one's life does not supply an autonomy-based argument for worker ownership, it may provide a utility-based argument. It is well known that lack of control generates stress and even physical illness. There is some evidence that worker-owners are happier than other employees (Kaswan, 2019), which implies an increase in total utility. The other arguments mentioned above are utility-based as well. Worker-owned enterprises appear to be more resilient (Olsen, 2013: Burdín, 2014; Palmer, 2019) and more productive (Pérotin, 2016) on average, although these outcomes are not guaranteed in any particular case. More egalitarian wages can also be a consideration. According to one report, the pay ratio of the highest to lowest earner in the Mondragon Corporation is about nine to one (Heales et al., 2017), while CEOs in the U.S. make 320 times as much as a typical worker (Mishel and Kandra, 2020). As noted in Chapter 3, the deontological basis for the utilitarian principle can support using equity criteria even when they do not maximize overall utility. One might also argue that greater equality in the workplace can boost total utility as well by improving worker morale.

In conclusion, the utilitarian potential of worker ownership deserves serious consideration when setting up a business corporation, if—and this is a big "if"—adequate financing can be obtained without ceding worker autonomy. When assessing utility, one must also take into account the legal environment, possible tax incentives, and past successes or failures of cooperative endeavors in the same industry.

6 Customer and employee relations

Codes of ethics

When an organization turns its attention to ethics, its first instinct is often to formulate a *code of ethics* or *code of conduct*. Such a code may be directed toward customers or employees, or both. It can reassure customers (and investors) that the company can be trusted, and it can clarify company policy for employees. Yet writing a code of ethics should be one of the later stages in the development of company ethics, not the first. Otherwise, the code is likely to consist of generalities or platitudes that provide little real guidance. An extreme example is Google's famous motto, "Don't be evil," although the company subsequently adopted a somewhat more helpful Code of Conduct (Alphabet, Inc., 2020). Ideally, a code should address specific types of conduct and represent the outcome of ethical reasoning and consensus building within the company.

The first step toward developing an ethical company is not to write an ethics code, but to build ethical competence in at least some of its managers and employees. This can be done through training workshops, an onboarding process, or hiring managers who have some ethics training in their background. The next step is to encourage open discussion of company policies from an ethical perspective, starting at the top. Managers and employees who have acquired analytical skills can include ethical reasoning in memos, meetings, and one-on-one dialog. This can signal to other managers and employees that it is OK to bring ethics into the conversation, in addition to providing examples of ethical analysis. Simply setting an example can be a powerful inducement and teaching tool. As issues are resolved, they can be codified in company memos and eventually incorporated into an ethics code that represents a culmination of the deliberative process, not the beginning. The code is most useful when it deals with specific situations in which employees are genuinely unsure about what is proper conduct. It can also clarify worker obligations under their employment contract by explicitly stating what the company expects.

A useful model for a company ethics code, with respect to level of detail if not company-specific content, is the Kodak Business Conduct Guide (Eastman Kodak Company, 2019). An example will illustrate its thoroughness. While Kodak employees should clearly avoid working against the interests of the company, they may be unsure whether this precludes owning stock in a competing company. The Business Conduct Guide has an answer. It begins by stating that an employee should not have a financial interest in an outside organization or individual "whose business may be affected by the employee's actions on behalf of Kodak." As for owning stocks, the Guide is precise; it is permissible to own securities that meet all of the following conditions:

- the securities are listed on a recognized stock exchange or traded on a regular over-the-counter basis;
- the combined holdings in the securities of the employee and his/her immediate family members are less than 1 percent of the company's outstanding securities; and
- the combined holdings of the securities of the employee and his/her immediate family members are relatively insubstantial in amount as a personal investment (pp. 6–7).

The phrase "relatively insubstantial" in the third condition is somewhat vague, but it is difficult to see how the company could define it more precisely in a practical and enforceable manner. The 22-page Guide states many other provisions with equal specificity and provides concrete examples to illustrate the rules.

Codes of ethics also play a key role in *professional ethics*. To see how, it is helpful to recall what a profession is. The word "profess" originally referred to vows taken by members of a religious order. This provides a clue to why we have professions and how they relate to ethics. When we check into a hospital, we benefit from the services of multiple physicians and nurses. It would be impossible to investigate each of these persons in advance to ascertain that they are competent in their field and practice it responsibly. Rather, we assume that because they belong to a medical or nursing profession, they have the necessary training and conduct themselves responsibly. By professing membership in their professions, doctors and nurses, in effect, *promise* that they will live up to the expectations the profession has created. Professional obligation is the obligation to keep this promise.

This means that determining professional obligation is really a question of fact: what has the profession led the public to expect from its members? Codes of ethics enter the picture at this point. They clarify the content of the professional promise by telling professionals how they should behave, and informing the public what they can expect from the profession. The most famous code of professional ethics in the Western world is the ancient Hippocratic Oath, which some medical schools still administer in modified form. The Oath is, of course, sorely inadequate for the complexities of modern medicine, but today we have medical codes of ethics that exhibit the kind of detail and precision that should characterize any professional code.

Business management is not ordinarily regarded as a profession in the sense discussed here, because there is no universally recognized set of expectations for managers, however desirable this might be. Yet one clearly recognized profession within the business world is accounting. Professionalism developed in this field because the essence of accounting is achieving transparency, which urgently requires transparent and well-defined reporting standards. The best-known codes of conduct are the International Financial Reporting Standards (IFRS), which originated in the European Union, and so-called Generally Accepted Accounting Standards (GAAP), one version of which is binding on public companies in the U.S. (where there is some recent movement away from GAAP toward IFRS). Professional associations in other business areas have issued standards, but frequent departures from these standards in practice make it difficult to say that they have established public expectations that would ground a specifically *professional* obligation to abide by the standards—which is not to say there is no *ethical* obligation to do so. For example, the European Advertising Standards Alliance and the American Advertising Federation have issued detailed codes of practice for advertising, partly motivated by a desire to avoid government mandates by encouraging self-regulation.

While there is no generally accepted code of ethics for business management in general, well-drafted codes in individual companies can serve as examples and may eventually lead to more broadly accepted standards. It was the pioneering work of Arthur Andersen and his accounting firm that, to a great degree, inspired professionalism in accounting. Ironically, the company he founded in 1913 collapsed 89 years later due to its involvement in the infamous Enron business scandal. The saga of how the firm gradually drifted away from the founder's principles provides an object lesson in how an organization can lose its ethical focus (Squires et al., 2003).

Pricing

Two of the most basic issues that arise in customer relations are product safety and product pricing. Chapter 4 discusses product safety at some depth in the context of two product liability case studies, and Chapter 5 deals with the related issue of whether it is ethical to sell harmful products such as cigarettes or unhealthy fast food. This section takes up the question of how product prices should be set.

The answer to the pricing question may appear to be simple: charge what the market will bear. Economics textbooks tell us that demand falls as prices rise. A merchant need only select a price that maximizes net income, which is the number of units sold multiplied by the contribution margin of each unit. In a competitive market, other sellers will arrive at about the same price because it is the one at which supply equals demand. Anyone who has ethical qualms about this natural market mechanism need only reflect on a fundamental theorem of welfare economics: the equilibrating price maximizes the sum of consumer surplus and producer surplus and thereby maximizes total welfare.

Even setting aside the idealistic market assumptions of this argument, it has little merit from an ethics perspective. First, the fact that prices arise from a "natural" market mechanism does not imply that they are ethical; any such inference would commit the naturalistic fallacy. Second, the argument seems to appeal to the utilitarian principle but incorrectly applies it. Even if we grant that equilibrated prices in the economy at large maximize net utility, this is irrelevant. What matters is whether an individual merchant's price is utility maximizing. This depends on the particular circumstances surrounding the merchant and the sale.

The fallacies in this argument notwithstanding, charging the market price is probably ethical in most everyday business situations. Raising or reducing the price relative to the going market rate would only transfer revenue from one merchant to another as buyers seek the lowest price. This is unlikely to increase net utility in most cases, partly because it complicates the logistics of price shopping. Charging the market price is generalizable as well, because the practice is, by definition, already generalized. Autonomy violation is normally not an issue.

However, there are special situations in which equilibrium pricing can be unethical. One is *price gouging* in times of temporary shortage. This sometimes occurs in a natural disaster, for example, when merchants may jack up the price of essential items like food, fuel, or portable electric generators because the market will bear it. In dire circumstances like these, the same limited number of items will be sold and utilized regardless of the price. This means that charging an inflated price only transfers wealth from economically devastated buyers to the seller, which is likely to reduce overall utility. Economists argue that scarce goods must be allocated somehow, and a price mechanism is an orderly way to do it. If charging high prices could actually avert a riot among customers who fight to be first in the queue, then there may be an argument here. Yet in most cases, simply selling the goods until they are exhausted is an "orderly" way to allocate them, and it has the advantage of creating greater utility than allocation by price. Of course, the utilitarian ideal is to allocate goods based on severity of need. This may be practical in some cases, as when health authorities distribute a scarce vaccine to medical personnel first because they are most likely to be exposed to disease. Yet merchants are generally not in a position to assess need and would find it impractical or illegal to favor certain customers in any event. For them, an ethical policy is simply to sell their wares at the normal market price until the shelves are empty, perhaps with restrictions on the quantity purchased by any individual, to prevent hoarding.

A related issue is posed by *surge pricing* algorithms used by ridesharing companies like Lyft and Uber. The algorithms raise rates when demand increases, usually during rush hour or holidays. This practice has been justified on the grounds that it incentivizes more drivers to make themselves available. This is a case where the economic argument is relevant to the utilitarian principle, because one company may have near-controlling influence over the market price in a given city. By tuning the pricing algorithm to simulate market equilibrium, a company can more or less maximize total producer and consumer surplus, thereby presumably maximizing utility. Yet this can lead to very high rates when demand spikes. On one much-cited occasion in the early days of ridesharing, Uber charged a minimum of Australian $100 per ride during a hostage crisis in Sydney, Australia. Even routine rush-hour demand can result in equilibrium prices that are unaffordable for most. Maximizing producer and consumer surplus in such cases may not maximize utility, because surplus is measured in money, and utility is not proportional to monetary gain or loss. Economically disadvantaged persons in urgent need of a ride may suffer much more from equilibrium pricing than drivers benefit. However, since drivers cannot judge who is in greatest need of a ride, the only visible alternative to allocation by price is to follow the example of popular restaurants that do not take reservations: to allocate by queuing and flexibility, so that customers willing to wait longer or be served at less popular times are more likely to be accommodated. This, however, removes the incentive for more drivers to participate, and potentially everyone is worse off. All things considered, the most reasonable utilitarian solution is perhaps to combine the two types of allocation. Ridesharing companies can use a certain amount of surge pricing, pass the higher prices on to drivers, and put a fairly low ceiling on how high the price can go.

Allocation by price can also be questioned when it comes to life's necessities. There seems to be a fairly broad, if by no means universal, consensus that everyone should have access to basic food, shelter, and medical care even when they cannot afford it. There is ethical grounding for this view, because deprivation of life's necessities is a violation of autonomy. A company's refusal to sell affordable cosmetics or cigarettes does not violate autonomy, even when it cuts off the supply to some people, because it does not interfere with customer action plans. As noted in Chapter 3, customers cannot have an action plan of being sold cosmetics and cigarettes, because they do not decide whether they are sold these items. However, if a refusal to provide affordable food or medical care cuts off its availability, it interferes with many ethical actions people can decide to undertake, because nourishment and health are necessary for almost any kind of action. This is a violation of autonomy.

While an individual company typically does not cut off availability of food or shelter by refusing to provide them at affordable prices, a pharmaceutical company might very well cut off the availability of life-saving drugs. This can occur in the U.S., for example, where companies often hold exclusive patent rights, and many people lack adequate medical insurance. In one dramatic case, Mylan Pharmaceuticals (which later merged with Upjohn to form Viatris) raised the price of its EpiPen six-fold after it acquired the rights to it from Merck in 2007. The EpiPen is a device that rapidly injects life-saving epinephrine into a person who is having a severe allergic reaction. There were complaints that, at a price of over $600 per pair, some families could not afford to have an EpiPen on hand for their children. This is despite the fact that the EpiPen's production cost is a tiny fraction of its price. In widely publicized testimony before a U.S. Congressional committee, Mylan CEO Heather Bresch defended the price in part by saying that, "in the complicated world of pharmaceutical pricing," many patients obtain EpiPens for a heavily discounted price, and Mylan collects only a fraction of the $600. Furthermore, much of this revenue must be invested in improving the device and "providing access to EpiPens in public places, starting with schools" (Bresch, 2016). Pharmaceutical pricing in the U.S. is indeed complex, so much so that probably no one fully understands it (Rosenthal, 2017). On top of this is the fact that pharmaceutical firms must finance research and development from sales revenues. Yet these firms create much of the pricing complexity themselves and can ascertain its impact on patients. The autonomy principle imposes on them an absolute obligation: they must ensure that their pricing policies do not deprive any single person of potential remedies for life-threatening or debilitating conditions.

Marketing and advertising

Marketing is often identified with advertising and sales promotion, but it has a broader purpose that is essential to any successful economy. That purpose is to match supply and demand, or more precisely, to determine what products and services the public needs or wants and is willing to purchase. Without this function, industry would generate a wasteful surplus of some products and create a shortage of others. While customer demand alone does not justify selling a harmful product (Chapter 5), it is important to determine which products are marketable so that a company can know its options.

All three ethical principles have a central role in marketing decisions. The utilitarian principle not only regulates decisions to sell existing products but has a bearing on the introduction of new ones. Some of the sharpest critiques of business over the years have targeted its use of advertising to create demand for frivolous products, resulting in needless resource consumption. While this is always a danger, one of the brightest spots in business is its ability to develop useful new product ideas, including those whose value may not be obvious at first. Ken Olsen, founder of Digital Equipment Corporation, famously predicted that "there is no reason anyone would want a computer in their home." At the other extreme, social media platforms seemed initially to be a major contribution to society, while their destructive effects have recently become clear (even if these effects may be due to how technology companies operate their platforms as much as to the concept itself). The checkered history of marketing counsels humility about our ability to predict the potential value of new products, and we must stand ready to modify or abandon products if things go sour.

The generalization principle is obviously relevant to one of the banes of marketing: false advertising. The legal definition of false advertising varies across jurisdictions. It is sometimes defined as false statements about the nature of the product itself, in which case someone pretending to be a doctor can endorse a patent medicine without being guilty of false advertising. In any event, an ethical evaluation boils down to whether the advertisement is deceptive, with respect to the product or anything else, and therefore ungeneralizable. As noted in Chapter 4, deception is causing someone to believe something you know is false. This means that overstatement of a product's virtues, known as "puffery" in the legal world, can be ethical even if it is untruthful. A pizza shop that advertises "the world's best pizza" deceives no one, because no one believes the claim. We expect a certain amount of exaggeration in advertising, except when specific product features are described.

The phenomenon of "advertising speech" goes far beyond advertising. Language is a complicated phenomenon with levels of subtlety, and statements that are literally false may serve a larger purpose without deception. A little well-intentioned flattery may be innocuous and non-deceptive even if it cannot be taken at face value. A car salesperson who falsely states, "this is the lowest price we can offer," does not necessarily mislead, if customers expect this kind of talk. It may only communicate that the salesperson cannot go much lower. "Signal jamming" that overstates financial health in a corporate report, while remaining within GAAP principles, may not mislead investors if they expect a slightly rosier-than-real picture (Kluger and Slezak, 2018). In the marketing domain, the general rule is that the ethical advertiser must be capable of believing rationally that an advertisement will cause no one to believe something false.

The autonomy principle is the hardest to apply to marketing but of central importance. Advertising has long been associated with subconscious, as opposed to rational, persuasion. This association began in earnest when Edward Bernays (1923) employed ideas introduced by his uncle, Sigmund Freud, while consulting with the advertising agency J. Walter Thomson. It was reinforced in the public mind when Vance Packard (1957) wrote of subliminal messages in advertising. His best-known example was the inclusion in a movie of popcorn images that went by too quickly for conscious awareness but boosted popcorn sales in cinemas (an idea that has since been debunked). This type of persuasion has the odor of autonomy violation, because it may circumvent rational faculties. One can imagine clear cases of such. Surreptitiously adding a drug to someone's food to induce reckless behavior is an undeniable violation of autonomy. Manipulative advertising is a less clear case, but we can check for autonomy violation by asking whether it interferes with ethical action plans without informed consent. If an addicted gambler has successfully tamed the impulse, but a casino's advertisement campaign overwhelms his ability to resist, we have interference with an existing action plan. However, if an advertisement for luscious chocolate cake on a restaurant table induces a patron to indulge, but the patron is not consciously following a low-calorie diet, there is no interference with an action plan. There is temptation, but no autonomy violation.

As for temptation, it is, of course, a regular feature of advertising, and its ethical assessment usually depends on the utilitarian consequences. Advertisements that result in an occasional indulgence can enhance utility by generating pleasure. Utilitarians are not opposed to hedonism, after all, as Jeremy Bentham was known to reduce all ethics to the maximization of pleasure. However, advertisements that lead to overindulgence and poor health, without a commensurate increase in pleasure, are disutilitarian and unethical.

Refusing service

An aspect of customer relations that has become quite controversial in recent years is refusal of service. To show how ethical principles might apply to this contentious issue, we consider two scenarios: refusing to cater a gay wedding, and refusing to serve a person who poses a health risk. Both of these denials of service are legally regulated in various ways, but for the sake of argument we suppose that they are legal and examine the underlying ethical arguments.

The Sweet Cakes Bakery in the U.S. state of Oregon refused to bake a wedding cake for a lesbian couple in 2013, on religious grounds. We can note straightaway that the refusal seems disutilitarian, because it embarrassed the couple and forced them to go to another bakery, with no compensating benefit to anyone. Given this, the refusal can be justified only if baking the cake violates some other ethical principle. It is not enough for the bakers to say that they believe gay marriage is wrong or that it is contrary to their religion. To make an ethical case, they must determine that contributing to a gay wedding actually violates an ethical principle.[1] Fully adjudicating such a claim is beyond the scope of a book on business ethics, but we can at least take note of what the bakers must show.

The bakers may respond that their refusal of service is actually utilitarian, because acting contrary to their beliefs would cause personal distress and

---

[1] This is not to deny that one can make a religious case without making an ethical case, since religions may self-consciously override ethical imperatives. Søren Kierkegaard considers "the teleological suspension of the ethical" as part of his discussion of the Biblical characters Abraham and Isaac in his classic work *Fear and Trembling* (1843). In any event, the question addressed here is the ethical one.

censure from their religious community, and these outweigh any incon-venience to the lesbian couple. If so, it is not only permissible but obliga-tory to refuse the sale, unless the refusal is ungeneralizable or a violation of autonomy. It is no violation of autonomy, even though it frustrates the couple's desire to do business with Sweet Cakes, because there is no interference with an ethical action plan. The couple cannot have an action plan of being sold a cake by this shop; they can decide only to purchase the cake if it is offered for sale.

However, one can mount a generalizability argument that may apply to a wide range of similar dilemmas. Let's suppose, for definiteness, that the bakers' action plan is to serve only customers of which they approve while sustaining a viable business. This may not be generalizable, because the market economy in which the bakers want to participate relies on the fact that buying and selling is based on quality and price, not on economically extraneous factors like sexual orientation. If shoppers had to go from one grocer or haberdasher to another in search of one that approves of their hairdo or accent, the market system as we know it would arguably not exist, and the bakers would not be able to sustain a viable business. It may be permissible to be selective in specialized services, as when archi-tects turn down projects that do not interest them. But when business is characterized by customers walking in off the street and buying a product, customers must be able to do just this. Selectivity may be generalizable when it is based on a recognized category of service, as when a restaurant posts a sign, "No shoes, no shirt, no service." This places the restaurant in a category where a certain dining ambience is provided, as opposed to a casual eatery on the beach. One might conclude from this argument, which is admittedly a bit strained, that discrimination against gay custom-ers is generalizable only if there are businesses that specialize in serving an established market niche for gay customers.

We do not address here the extent to which governments should discour-age discrimination, but the legal environment is relevant to an individual merchant's decision. As it happens, Oregon's Equality Act bans discrimi-nation on the basis of sexual orientation, and a judge ordered Sweet Cakes Bakery to pay the gay couple $135,000 in damages. A legal prohibition of this sort not only raises the utilitarian cost of refusing service, but it imposes at least a prima facie obligation to serve all paying customers, because violation of the law is normally ungeneralizable. The bakers may argue that their refusal is justified as civil disobedience, because they view the law to be immoral. The ethical status of civil disobedience has been debated for centuries, going back at least to Sophocles' play *Antigone*, in which the title character defies the law by giving her brother a proper burial. While it has been argued that a civilly disobedient individual must be willing to accept the penalty for non-compliance (Rawls, 1971), the bakers were evidently willing to do so. They could therefore argue that civil disobedience was justified in their case, but only if they can rationally defend their claim that the Equality Act is immoral.

During the Covid-19 pandemic that struck the world in 2020, many places of business required customers to wear a protective mask while shopping. This was often in response to a government order, or simply part of an effort to protect employees and other customers from infection. Remarkably, there were many reports of threats and violence against employees who asked customers to wear a mask. A security guard in a U.S. retail store was fatally shot after making such a request (Snyder et al., 2020), and passengers boarding a bus in France beat the driver to death when he asked them to do the same (BBC, 2020). Obviously it is wrong to attack employees, but the issue here is whether a business should refuse service to maskless customers. Defiant customers typically insist that mask requirements restrict their freedom, but there is no violation of autonomy in refusing to serve them. There is no interference with an ethical action plan, because customers cannot have an action plan of being served while not wearing a mask. This is not their choice to make, and even if it is, the action plan is unethical. It is disutilitarian to subject staff and customers to a risk of infection that is easily mitigated by the slight inconvenience of wearing a mask, particularly since even asymptomatic individuals can spread the virus. The store's utility calculation, however, is less clear, because a mask-wearing requirement could trigger a violent reaction. A utilitarian compromise is perhaps to offer recalcitrant customers a mask and suggest politely that they wear it, for the safety of themselves and others, without denying service if they refuse.

An issue of civil disobedience can arise here as well, at least when the store is following a government mask order. Maskless customers frequently claim that they are protesting what they see as an unjust government intrusion on their personal freedom. One can in principle make such a case, but it is incumbent on the defiant customer to show that a mask mandate in the midst of a pandemic is unjust.

Job search

We now turn our attention from customers to employees. One becomes an employee by obtaining a *job*, which is an extended engagement with a company that entitles the employee to certain legal rights. While temporary and contract workers are a rapidly increasing phenomenon, most workers in developed economies earn their livelihood through employment. This makes securing a job a top priority that can induce job seekers to cut ethical corners, such as résumé padding and reneging on an employment contract.

Résumé padding is the practice of exaggerating or even fabricating qualifications for a job, presumably when it is difficult for the prospective employer to verify the claims. Business students in the job market sometimes defend résumé padding on the grounds that "everybody does it." The practice is allegedly non-deceptive because employers expect a certain amount of embellishment, a lack of which could itself be deceptive because it causes the employer to underestimate the applicant relative to others. Experience teaches that when people say everybody does it, almost certainly not everyone does it, but we can suppose for the sake of argument that résumé padding is widely practiced. This could, in principle, lead to a type of signal jamming that deceives no one and is therefore generalizable.

The problem with this line of argument is showing that a given type of exaggeration is non-deceptive. Let's suppose that it is well known that business school graduates routinely overstate the responsibilities they held during summer internships. While they did little more than make coffee while sitting in on meetings, the résumé might say that they "worked with an international marketing team." If few applicants are frank about their lack of responsibility in such cases, one might argue that this particular type of padding is innocuous and non-deceptive. This, however, does not show that padding of any sort is non-deceptive, even when it is of minor importance. It does not show that a one-hour paint job can be described as "volunteer work with Habitat for Humanity" without misleading the employer, when there is no well-known and established practice of overstating volunteer work. The ethical option in such cases is for the résumé to highlight the applicant's unique strengths relative to others (and everyone has such strengths) rather than exaggerate less convincing qualifications. This not only avoids a risk that the employer will underestimate the honest candidate's abilities, but allows for a better fit between applicants and jobs, a utilitarian advantage.

Reneging on an employment contract poses a more perplexing dilemma, partly because there are so many ways to rationalize a decision to renege. The dilemma arises all too often because (a) business students interview with several companies during a recruiting season, (b) job offers come at unpredictable times and may be attached to tight deadlines for a response, and (c) companies typically ask for a commitment weeks or months before the student actually starts work. As a result, an attractive offer may come along after the student has already signed with another company. Perhaps the most frequently heard justification for reneging is legal in nature: there are ways to escape legal obligation under the employment contract, or the employer will not take any legal action if there is breach of contract. Yet even when walking away from a contract is legal, it may be unethical. From an ethical perspective, the primary function of signing a contract is that it signals a firm commitment on both sides. It means that the applicant really is promising to work for the company, and the company really is promising to employ the applicant.

Rather than rehearse other rationalizations, let's go directly to an application of ethical principles. Utilitarian considerations are sometimes relevant. Reneging may incur substantial cost to a company, while the employee only gains a somewhat larger salary. For example, the company might suffer significant losses when it must delay a project in order to reopen the search for a key member of the team. This would make it unethical to renege. At the other extreme, sticking with a contract may cause the employee to pass up a life-changing opportunity, when the company is scarcely impacted by whether the position is immediately filled. The latter situation provides an oft-cited utilitarian argument for reneging, but generalizability must be considered as well.

The possible lack of generalizability is, of course, the linchpin of the issue and the reason people often feel uneasy about reneging. They know they are breaking a promise, and they know they would be outraged if the company reneged on them. Some say that while it may be unpleasant to break a promise, it should be treated simply as a business decision—as though promises had nothing to do with business. The very possibility of business, of course, rests on promises. The root problem with breaking an employment agreement is that a general practice of doing so would undermine the possibility of making such agreements. Job seekers want the company to follow through when it promises a job, but the employer would see no point in entering into an agreement if it means nothing to the other party. The applicant would have no option but to show up on the first day of work and hope the job is still there, and the employer would have no option but to wait and see if anyone shows up. Employment could proceed in this fashion, but it would not be a system in which job seekers could plan ahead by moving to a new address, or in which employers could count on having certain staff available. If the job seeker's action plan is to take advantage of an employer's promise of a job unless a better offer comes along, then that action plan is ungeneralizable and unethical. A plan to keep looking for a job in hope of finding a better one, after already signing with a company, is ungeneralizable and unethical for similar reasons.

More complex action plans can be generalizable, however, assuming they are legal. One might plan to honor a certain employment contract unless an unforeseen family situation arises, such as the necessity of caring for an ailing parent in another city. This is clearly generalizable, as such exceptions would not undermine a job market with employment contracts. The most difficult dilemma arises when that dream job unexpectedly materializes after one has already signed with another company. The utilitarian advantage of accepting it is clear, since employees are more productive and companies are more successful when people love their jobs, and employees who turn down their dream job may be demoralized and soon leave the company anyway. Reneging may be generalizable in such cases, if "dream job" is narrowly enough defined (in advance, not after the offer arrives) that it is quite unusual for one to come along after signing. This again assumes that there is a legal way to renege. The ideal, of course, would be for both parties to abandon the contract by mutual consent, as when the employer would rather recruit someone else than have a demoralized employee on board.

Employment and the gig economy

Perhaps the most fundamental ethical issues in employment are the extent to which a firm is obligated to provide steady employment, a living wage with benefits, and good working conditions. The next section deals with working conditions. The first two issues are posed by the rapidly growing gig economy, and we address them in this specific context rather than try to resolve them in general.

The *gig economy* is the sector of the economy that relies on temporary workers rather than employees. Some temporary workers are *contract workers*, who enter into contracts directly with a company and submit their own invoices for services rendered. They range from highly paid professionals to low-paid retail clerks. Others are *contingent workers*, who are recruited by a temporary employment agency. They often have few legal protections, must make do with unsteady work, and receive as wages only a fraction of what the agency is paid for their work. By contrast, *employees* have an ongoing relationship with the company for which they work, are bound by company rules, and enjoy legal protections that vary widely across jurisdictions. The legal protections might include minimum wage laws, provisions for overtime pay, family and medical leave benefits, and some protection against arbitrary dismissal.

In the 1920s, *gigs* were temporary engagements for jazz musicians. Today, gigs in a more general sense make up a significant portion of national economies. At least 36 percent of U.S. workers participate in the gig economy, and 5–10 percent of workers rely on it for their primary means of support (U.S. Bureau of Labor Statistics, 2018). About 12 percent of workers in Organisation for Economic Co-operation and Development countries are dependent on temporary work, including 5 percent in the United Kingdom, 12 percent in Germany, 16 percent in France, and 29 percent in Colombia (Organisation for Economic Co-operation and Development, 2020). The gig economy is often associated with online apps like Uber and TaskRabbit, but they account for only a small portion of this sector. Employers have been quietly shifting to contingent workers for tasks previously done in-house, such as janitorial duties, bartending in coffee shops, hotel housekeeping, and health care (where they are sometimes known as *locum tenens*, or substitutes). Temporary work offers multiple advantages to employers and correlative disadvantages to workers. There are generally no fringe benefits, overtime pay, or paid sick leave. The laborious paperwork of hiring and firing is avoided, and workers can be on site the next day rather than after a lengthy recruiting process. Some of the uncertainty of the business cycle is shifted to labor, since the company can simply request fewer workers when demand temporarily slackens rather than carry along unneeded employees. While temporary workers may enjoy more freedom than employees, the stress of uncertain employment exacts a toll on psychological and physical health. Most of all, contingent workers tend to earn significantly lower wages than employees. In one striking example, a medical transcriptionist saw her wages drop from $19 to $6 an hour when her employer required her to work for an outside transcription service, even though she did the same work at the same desk (Vinik, 2018).

An ethical question facing many companies is whether they should replace employees with contingent workers to reap these advantages. Provided there is no violation of law or contract, it is not obvious why such a move would be ungeneralizable, as it is rapidly being generalized. The dominant factor is the utilitarian calculation, since outsourcing reduces the net utility of workers and disrupts the lives of dismissed employees. If the main financial effect of such a move is to transfer wealth from workers to stockholders, then it is disutilitarian, since one group loses more utility than the other gains. While the company must honor its fiduciary duty to stockholders, there is no duty to take an unethical action on their behalf, as we have discussed. On the other hand, market conditions are increasingly forcing companies to outsource in order to compete with others doing the same. If a company fails to take action, it may have to resort to layoffs. In such cases, outsourcing is probably the lesser of two evils and becomes the utilitarian choice.

Working conditions

The ethical arguments that surround working conditions are best introduced in the context of a real example. At various times, the online retailer Amazon has required its warehouse workers to queue up before going home in order to be searched for pilfered merchandise. The workers are not paid for the time consumed by these searches, which they say is close to half an hour each day. This practice gave rise to a number of lawsuits, and the issue was finally appealed to the U.S. Supreme Court in 2014. The Court ruled that Amazon has no obligation under Federal law to compensate workers for the time (Liptak, 2014). Yet the lawsuits continued, based on alleged violations of individual state laws. Most recently, Amazon settled for about $11 million in a suit brought by California warehouse workers, after Apple lost a similar case in the California Supreme Court (Clark, 2020).

A company should, of course, follow the law in such cases, but let's suppose that failure to compensate workers has not been ruled illegal. We are interested in Amazon's ethical obligation. A frequent response to dilemmas of this sort is, "if workers don't like company policy, they are free to work somewhere else." While we can grant that workers are "free" to work elsewhere, at least if another job is available, it is unclear how this claim resolves the ethical issue. It is only a factual claim, and an ethical principle is needed to draw the desired conclusion without violating the is-ought gap (Chapter 2).

One interpretation of the argument is that Amazon's policy is ethical because it does not violate autonomy. The argument is invalid, of course, because one must show that the policy conforms to other ethical principles as well. Yet there appears, in fact, to be no autonomy violation, because there is no interference with an ethical action plan. Workers cannot have an action plan of being paid to undergo searches, because this is not their decision to make. There could be an autonomy violation if a worker has no means of support other than a job at Amazon. Cutting off the only means of support interferes with many ethical action plans and is therefore an autonomy violation. Furthermore, threatening to violate autonomy, unless one performs some action, is itself a violation of autonomy; one who hands over his wallet at gunpoint suffers an autonomy violation. Yet we will grant that this is not the situation here, since workers can usually find some minimal means of support (from relatives if necessary) if fired from Amazon. There seems to be no compelling case for a violation of autonomy.

One might attempt to complete the defense of Amazon's policy by showing it is consistent with the generalization and utilitarian principles as well. Compliance with generalizability requires, in particular, that the policy is legal and breaches no agreement with employees. We are supposing for the sake of argument that it is legal. We can suppose further that this is a case of *employment-at-will*, meaning that the company can dismiss an employee at any time, for any reason or no reason, without any violation of law or contract. Yet there may be an implicit agreement with employees that, while not legally enforceable, is binding ethically. Suppose, for example, that Amazon tells a warehouse worker that she must babysit the boss's kids during work hours, or else be fired. A worker might reasonably expect to be inconvenienced by normal business decisions, such as relocating the warehouse to another city. Or she might expect to be dismissed if the company experiences poor sales, restructuring, or a move to automation. These expectations are perhaps implicit in the employment agreement. Yet someone hired as a warehouse worker cannot reasonably expect babysitting duties. Amazon might concede this point but insist that employees can most certainly expect security searches. The policy at issue, however, is a time-consuming search without compensation. It is a well-established convention that when one is paid by the hour, one is paid for the time one must be at work. Employees can certainly expect a brief security check before clocking in, since this is common in workplaces, but not a 30-minute delay after clocking out. The matter therefore reduces to a question of fact: when Amazon hired its warehouse workers, could they reasonably assume that they would be paid for time they are required to be at work? The flurry of lawsuits in response to Amazon's policy suggests that this is, in fact, a reasonable expectation. If so, the policy is ungeneralizable and unethical. Of course, if lengthy unpaid searches were the norm at Amazon before any of today's workers were hired, this argument would not apply, since everyone would expect detention after work.

As for the utilitarian principle, it is difficult to see how transferring a half-hour's pay from workers to the company's coffers could be utilitarian. It would be one thing if Amazon were strapped for cash, but it is a highly prosperous company with $887 billion market capitalization, run by the richest man in the world. Beyond this, the policy inspires employee resentment, particularly when the necessity to prevent pilferage already indicates a serious morale problem. Resentment, in turn, leads to management problems and less productivity, which harms employees, stockholders, and customers alike. Amazon has the resources to realize a much more positive vision of enlightened management. It has begun to move in this direction by providing partially subsidized health insurance, limited paid time off and holiday overtime wages, and unpaid parental leave.

Under intense public pressure, the company raised its U.S. minimum wage to $15 per hour (Chappell and Wamsley, 2018). Yet its sick leave policy and health-related working conditions remain controversial, particularly during the Covid-19 pandemic (Palmer, 2020). The greatest utilitarian potential of the work force has yet to be realized, because employees who know they are valued contribute more to the company. One approach is to take a cue from Toyota and other Japanese firms by harnessing worker ideas. As Amazon installs artificial intelligence-driven robots in its warehouses (there are already 200,000 of them), workers can assist in the machines' learning process, as well as help design a warehouse in which humans and machines can work together efficiently. While robots can lead to technological unemployment, as we discuss in Chapter 7, one way to address this problem is to use machines to augment human capabilities rather than try to duplicate them (Hooker and Kim, 2019, 2020). One of the chief contributions that business can make to human welfare is to allow employees to realize their full intellectual and creative potential, as this not only enhances work life but leads to greater productivity and better ideas.

Whistle blowing

Some of the most vexing dilemmas in business ethics arise when employees feel an obligation to "blow the whistle" on unethical activity in the company. Whistle blowing can be internal or external, depending on whether the inappropriate behavior is reported to company managers or to the public. The questionable behavior can range from minor expense account padding to major malfeasance that endangers lives. The dilemmas are hard because the consequences are highly unpredictable. Whistle blowers can suffer retaliation and even sacrifice their mental and physical health, while their efforts may be futile.

Low-profile whistle-blowing situations commonly arise when co-workers or bosses exaggerate their travel expenses to receive a larger reimbursement. It is not unusual for colleagues to tell a new staff member that expense padding is routine in the company and even viewed by managers as a fringe benefit. To examine some of the relevant ethical arguments, let's suppose that an employee learns that a colleague is requesting reimbursement for restaurant meals with potential clients, when some of the meals are actually get-togethers with family or friends. A duty to report this behavior might derive from either the generalization or the utilitarian principle.

Generalizability comes into play if reporting is required by the employment agreement. Certainly the employee should speak up if it is part of her job description to certify or audit expense reports, but this is normally not the case. Reporting is also contractually required if it is explicitly mentioned in the company's code of conduct. Absent this, however, it is difficult to find a generalizability problem with minding one's own business. To run a generalization test, we can suppose that the employee's primary reason for remaining quiet is that she wants to avoid any risk to her career. We can now ask if she could accomplish this if it were universal practice for staff to overlook such minor infractions by colleagues. It seems very likely that she could, because it is already probably quite unusual for employees to point a finger when it might endanger their career to do so. Companies operate successfully in spite of this, because they generally have audit procedures that prevent expense padding from getting out of hand.

The utilitarian principle is by far the more challenging to apply, because revealing malfeasance has unpredictable consequences. The primary risk is to the whistle blower herself. Co-workers may resent informers and retaliate by mentioning certain "deficiencies" in her work to managers. This may lead to a mediocre annual performance review and even a dismissal with the company's next reduction in force. Many companies offer anonymous hotlines for reporting unethical behavior, but one cannot be certain they are truly anonymous. The human resources staff may put two and two together and deduce who tipped them off. Distressingly, the whistle blower may take these risks for nothing. Managers may overlook the reported dishonesty because the accused is a "rainmaker" (i.e., someone who brings in lucrative contracts). Or, the company may actually tolerate expense padding as some co-workers claim. When it is impossible to weigh personal risk against possible company benefit in a reasonable fashion, inaction satisfies the utilitarian principle by default. The principle requires taking action only when rationality requires one to believe that doing so enhances net utility. Of course, there are cases where the potential damage clearly outweighs personal risk. A flight attendant who sees a pilot drinking heavily before a flight must speak up.

Similar issues arise in large-scale whistle blowing. Management may not take warnings seriously, as apparently occurred during production of the Boeing 737 Max (Marsh and Wallace, 2019). The aircraft was later grounded worldwide after two crashes killed everyone on board. Whistle blowers and their families can also suffer serious repercussions. A cautionary tale is provided by the most famous whistle-blowing case in the annals of business ethics. Roger Boisjoly warned in 1986 that O-rings could fail during the launch of the Space Shuttle *Challenger* (Boisjoly et al., 1989). His warnings were ignored, and the craft exploded before a worldwide television audience 73 seconds after launch, killing the seven crew members. Boisjoly later told his story to a Congressional committee. He also paid a price. He was shunned by company managers and neighbors, blacklisted by employers, and obliged to collect disability benefits due to posttraumatic stress disorder. As he put it, the experience "destroyed my career, my life, everything else," although he later received awards for his courage. This is not to suggest that whistle blowing is never justified in high-profile cases. Roger Boisjoly did the right thing. It does remind us, however, that one should not underestimate the personal hazards of going public.

7   Ethics and technology

Artificial intelligence and machine learning

Recent years have seen an epoch-making change in technology. It has ushered in what some call the Second Machine Age (Brynjolfsson and McAfee, 2014) or the Fourth Industrial Revolution (Schwab, 2016). The first three revolutions were the introduction of steam and water power in the eighteenth century, the development of electricity and efficient production in the late nineteenth century, and the advent of computers in the late twentieth century. The twenty-first century brings us artificial intelligence (AI), robotics, biotechnology, and an array of innovations based on the Internet and other advances in communications. These technologies pose new and vexing ethical dilemmas as well as lending new urgency to old ones. Nearly all of these issues have major implications for business practice.

Perhaps the most-discussed dilemmas are those connected with AI, and in particular the use of AI for decision making. While earlier industrial revolutions displaced manual or clerical labor, the most recent revolution displaces decision makers. The technology is based primarily on two ideas: deep learning in artificial neural networks, and to a lesser extent, classification by support vector machines.

It is important for ethical purposes to understand basically how these technologies work, and in particular that they are not magic, despite the hype than often surrounds them. An *artificial neural network* is essentially a way of fitting mathematical functions to data, much as statisticians do in classical regression. Elementary linear regression, for example, plots a line through data points on a graph so as to capture, as closely as possible, the functional relationship revealed by the points. A neural network consists of many functions, rather than just one as in classical regression, that are associated conceptually with nodes of a layered network. The nodes receive inputs from the previous layer and mathematically convert them to outputs transmitted to the next layer, in a fashion inspired by synapses in a biological neural network. The functions are adjusted to "learn" relationships revealed by data in a training set, much as a regression line is adjusted to "learn" the relationship implied by points on a graph. The learning mechanism is nothing more than a mathematical procedure ("back propagation") that computes the best fit.

A breakthrough in neural networks occurred when investigators began to realize that networks with multiple layers (rather than three as in early work) are far more effective at recognizing patterns, basically because the amount of information they can store increases exponentially with the number of layers. This gave rise to so-called *deep learning*, where the adjective "deep" refers simply to the larger number of layers in the network. Today, properly trained neural networks can drive cars, recognize images (including human faces), interpret medical scans, screen job applicants, filter social networking posts, detect credit card fraud, and carry out a host of other relatively high-level tasks. A much-discussed application is to the processing of mortgage loan applications. The neural network takes the applicant's personal and financial information as input and, as output, recommends for or against granting the loan, or perhaps estimates the probability of default. The network is trained on a historical data set that contains, for a large number of loan recipients, their personal and financial data along with whether they repaid the loan. This kind of training presumably teaches the network to recognize features that predict repayment.

A serious technical problem with this and other applications is "overfitting," a phenomenon well known to statisticians. Because so many functions are fitted to the data, the network is very good at learning patterns in a given training set, but it may learn too many patterns. It may pick up features that happen to correlate with the desired output in one data set but have no relevance in general. In one famous example, a neural network trained to recognize images worked very well on the training set but mistook a school bus for an ostrich when a few pixels were changed in the photo. Designing *supervised learning* techniques that overcome this problem is a major research area in the field.

Support vector machines, which are very different from neural networks, classify by geometrically separating "yes" points from "no" points. For example, if the features of loan applicants in the training set are plotted as points (vectors) in multidimensional space, a support vector machine is a hyperplane (multidimensional plane) that best separates points representing those who repaid from the remaining points. A new applicant receives a loan if the point representing his or her features lies on the "yes" side of the hyperplane. Sophisticated "kernel" techniques allow one to separate points with curved surfaces as well as flat hyperplanes.

Bias in machine learning

The most widely recognized ethical problem with machine learning is that it may result in *bias* against minority or disadvantaged groups. The widespread attention stems in part from a desire to comply with anti-discrimination laws, and a vast literature has emerged in a few short years. The mortgage loan decision is a well-known case in point. Difficulties begin when the machine discovers that members of, say, a minority ethnic group are more likely to default on mortgage loans. Individuals in the minority group may be denied a loan even when it would be granted to a member of the dominant ethnic group with the same financial characteristics. This outcome is frequently seen as unfair. Removing ethnic data from the training set does not solve the problem, because other attributes may correlate with ethnicity. The fact that one lives in a low-income neighborhood may allow the machine to infer a high risk of default, because financially irresponsible individuals tend to live in low-income neighborhoods. Yet members of an ethnic minority may also live in low-income neighborhoods, due to social factors that have nothing to do with financial responsibility. This can result in bias against members of the minority group.

The AI community has addressed this issue by proposing a number of metrics to determine whether a machine classifies fairly. If it does not, the supervised training procedure is adjusted in an attempt to achieve fairness. However, there are many different ways to measure fairness, with no consensus on why one should choose one rather than another. One popular website catalogs no fewer than 70 fairness metrics (IBM, 2020).

We briefly describe here the best-known metrics, while a brief mathematical treatment can be found in the Appendix.

The AI literature draws a general distinction between "individual fairness" and "group fairness," the latter often called "statistical fairness." *Individual fairness* says roughly that relevantly similar individuals should be treated similarly (Dwork et al., 2012). Yet this principle is fundamentally unclear. How similar must individuals be to receive the same classification? If a loan applicant from a protected group has 25 percent less in assets than a non-protected applicant who is granted a loan, one must decide whether this is close enough to say "yes," and why. The task of defining relevant similarity is essentially the same as the original task of identifying financial criteria that qualify one for a loan. If we know how to do this, we do not need machine learning in the first place.

Statistical fairness measures are well defined but raise problems of their own. It is most convenient to express them in terms of probabilities. The probability that an AI system will *select* a member of a given group (e.g., by granting a loan) is the fraction of persons in the group who would be selected if evaluated, and likewise for other probabilities. This is generally different from the fraction of people who are truly qualified for selection, because any classification system is subject to errors. The aim is to ensure that selection decisions are not biased against a particular group. The chief statistical fairness measures are as follows.

- *Demographic parity* requires that the probability of being selected is the same for members of a protected group as for everyone else. This is a very strict measure. For example, it rules out selecting a greater fraction of protected persons even if they are more highly qualified for selection than the general population.
- *Equalized odds* requires that (a) the probability of selecting a protected person who is qualified is the same as selecting a non-protected person who is qualified, and (b) the probability of selecting a protected person who is not qualified is the same as selecting a non-protected person who is not qualified (Zafar et al., 2017). A weaker form of the metric is *equality of opportunity*, which requires only (a) (Hardt et al., 2016). These metrics avoid one of the weaknesses of demographic parity, because they always allow selecting exactly those who are qualified. However, both metrics can allow a very few protected persons

to be selected, if relatively few are qualified due to social and historical factors. This can be corrected by affirmative action, discussed below.

- *Predictive rate parity* is the converse of equalized odds. It requires that the probability of selecting a qualified person in the protected group is the same as selecting a qualified person in the non-protected group, and similarly for non-qualified persons (Zafar et al., 2017). This again allows a very few protected persons to be selected, so long as those few selected are as likely to be qualified as other selected persons.

- *Counterfactual fairness* seems closely related to the intuition that inspires fairness measures, but it is difficult to assess. It requires that the probability of selecting a person who belongs to a protected class would have been the same in an alternative world in which that person belongs to an unprotected class. It is unclear what this kind of counterfactual statement even means, as there are deep philosophical problems with the interpretation of counterfactuals in general (e.g., Lewis, 2001). The proposers of counterfactual fairness (Kusner et al., 2017; Russell et al., 2017) give an interpretation in terms of underlying causes. Suppose that the protected class is a minority race, and that the likelihood of repaying a mortgage depends on an underlying characteristic of financial responsibility that cannot be directly observed. Financial responsibility obviously has no causal influence on one's race, but either race or financial irresponsibility may cause one to live in a low-income neighborhood. Individuals of a minority race may therefore be denied loans due to their residence in a low-income neighborhood, even when they are financially responsible. Counterfactual fairness requires that the loan decision would have been the same if it were based only on the unobserved characteristic of financial responsibility. The influence of this unobserved characteristic, and whether an individual possesses the characteristic, must somehow be statistically inferred from what can be observed, and this is a challenging task. Kusner et al. use Bayesian inference in causal networks for this purpose (Pearl, 2000; Pearl et al., 2016).

The proliferation of attempts to make fairness precise is due to the inherent vagueness of the concept (Chapter 2). Even the academic literature gives it a wide range of interpretations (Binns, 2018). Rather than wrestle with the concept, it is more productive to address the ethical issues directly. Perhaps the most fundamental issue is whether one should even try to select precisely those individuals who are qualified, or whether one should tip the scales in favor of a protected group. This is obviously a major social issue that has been addressed by government policies ranging from India's "scheduled classes," to Malaysia's quotas for the Indigenous Bumiputera population, to "affirmative action" hiring procedures in the U.S. It concerns business firms as well, particularly in hiring decisions.

It is important to distinguish a stronger and weaker sense of preferential treatment. Returning to the example of mortgage lending, applicants can be given priority in the strong sense just suggested, by relaxing the qualifications for receiving a loan. But they could also receive priority in the weaker, less controversial sense of simply correcting an estimation flaw in the machine learning procedure. If there is reason to believe that machine learning underestimates the probability that a minority applicant will repay the loan, then the minority status could be explicitly considered as a means to correct this kind of bias. This weaker type of preference clearly creates more utility than no preference at all, because it results in a more efficient allocation of capital. Defaults on loans are bad for everyone, and a more accurate estimate of repayment probability results in fewer defaults. This provides support for both equalized odds and predictive rate parity.

The stronger kind of preference awards loans to some minority applicants who are less deserving on the merits than majority applicants. Arguments for a general social practice of this sort are deep and complex, usually referring to the necessity of correcting a historical wrong without triggering a counterproductive backlash. A simpler utilitarian argument, however, might apply to an individual company. Granting a loan to a less qualified minority applicant could create greater expected utility than granting it to a more qualified majority applicant, because the latter has a greater probability of obtaining a loan elsewhere or at a later time. This assumes, of course, that the higher risk of default for the minority applicant is not so great as to offset this advantage. A policy of this kind is generally inconsistent with equalized odds and predictive rate parity. It could satisfy demographic parity if the preferential treatment of minorities is adjusted to achieve it, although the utilitarian argument does not support this particular outcome. It only supports preferential treatment to the extent that it maximizes utility, which could still result in disproportionately few minority applicants receiving loans, or even disproportionately many.

The generalization principle is equally relevant to AI-based decision making and has implications for counterfactual fairness in particular. In the case of mortgage loans, the most obvious application of generalizability arises if we suppose there is an implied agreement between a loan applicant and the bank. The applicant invests considerable time and effort in applying for a loan, divulging substantial data about personal finances, perhaps on the assumption that the bank will make a determination on the basis of credit worthiness alone. It is hard to see how the bank could honor such an agreement without complying with some form of counterfactual fairness.

At this point, we can sum up the ethical situation of mortgage loans as follows:

- Preferential treatment in the weak sense (taking into account protected status to correct for predictive bias) is generalizable and can increase utility. It is ethically obligatory, unless the stronger sense of preferential treatment is generalizable and creates still greater utility. Weak preferential treatment satisfies equalized odds, predictive rate parity, and counterfactual fairness, while it may or may not satisfy demographic fairness.
- Preferential treatment in the strong sense (selecting some protected individuals who are less than qualified) can be utilitarian, and if so it is ethically obligatory unless it violates the implied agreement between applicant and lender and is ungeneralizable for this reason. Strong preferential treatment generally violates equalized odds, predictive rate parity, and counterfactual fairness, while it may or may not satisfy demographic fairness.

Much of this analysis rides on the content of an implied agreement, which is a question of fact (not ethics) that depends on the social and psychological context. Yet we can at least observe that the root issue in AI fairness is not one of finding the correct fairness metric. It is a matter of determining what kind of preferential treatment is obligatory, if any, based on the generalization and utilitarian principles. Once this is settled, one can select a fairness metric that is consistent with ethics.

Teaching ethics to machines

We want machines to make ethical decisions, not only by maintaining statistical fairness in the appropriate sense, but in other ways as well. The AI community frequently refers to the task of designing an ethical machine as *value alignment*, which has the goal of aligning the machine's values with human values. Yet there is a fundamental ambiguity in what is meant by "values." The term could refer to what humans take to be desirable or preferable, or to ethical values: what is actually right and wrong. The former is a question of fact and the latter is a question of principle. As noted in Chapter 2, the two types of question must be addressed in very different ways: by empirical observation on the one hand, and by analysis on the other. There is a danger of trading on this ambiguity, because value alignment is normally conducted, at least in part, by inferring "values" from observed human behavior and opinions that are assembled into a large training set. One cannot arrive at valid ethical principles from such observations without committing the naturalistic fallacy.

The best-known value alignment problem is perhaps that imposed by designing a self-driving car. To deal with this problem, the MIT Media Lab gathered over 30 million opinions regarding various driving dilemmas from more than 180 countries, with the goal of creating a "Moral Machine" (MIT Media Lab, 2020). Investigators at the lab analyzed these data to develop "a computational model of how the human mind arrives at a decision in a moral dilemma" (Kim et al., 2018: 202). Unfortunately, most of the driving situations posed were trolley car-style dilemmas (Foot, 1967; Thomson, 1976) in which the driver must decide between running over one person rather than another, dilemmas that are very rare and about which few drivers are likely to have a meaningful opinion. Yet one could, in principle, query drivers in different countries about how to deal with more realistic situations and thereby teach a car how to behave itself appropriately in each country. One might argue that this does not commit the naturalistic fallacy, because the inference involves an ethical premise: a car should adhere to local driving norms, perhaps for the utilitarian reason that violating those norms could cause an accident.

Suppose, however, that some of the observed norms are ethically suspect, such as yielding the right of way only to members of the dominant ethnic group, or driving at high speed through a slum neighborhood where kids play in the street. In fact, one of the designers of the Moral Machine later stated, "A word of warning: the preferences we found are not meant to instruct car programmers as to how they *should* regulate AVs [autonomous vehicles]...The public can be ill-informed and biased, and some of the preferences we report are troubling" (Awad, 2019, original emphasis). At some point, independently derived ethical principles must be applied to avoid teaching the machine bad behavior. This is not to say that local preferences are irrelevant to the application of principles. In some countries, for example, one is expected to wait for a gap in the traffic before pulling onto a main thoroughfare, while in other countries one can edge out into the traffic stream as others yield somewhat. It is important to be aware of the local convention before deciding what kind of driving is ethical, perhaps on utilitarian grounds. However, one cannot infer the ethical principle itself solely from observed preferences. Such mechanisms as neural networks or support vector machines can learn only what is generally practiced or regarded as appropriate, not what is ethical.

The question remains, then, as to how one can teach ethics to a machine. One possibility is to apply ethics during supervised learning, by screening out unethical observed preferences. Yet ethical principles must be applied to action plans, not merely to behavior or preferences. The action in question must be accompanied by a rationale that indicates the circumstances under which the action is taken. Furthermore, as noted in Chapter 3, the rationale must be in its most general form before subjected to ethical tests. It is often unclear how to convert a specific observed preference to a general action plan. Ethical screening of a neural network's output is equally problematic. It is even less clear how to convert the output to an action plan, as it results from a specific driving situation encountered on the road. The most satisfactory approach is to control an autonomous vehicle with action plans from the start, where those action plans have been subjected to ethical tests in advance. Fortuitously, the if-then form of action plans is already well suited for coded instructions. Deep learning can then be used to identify which action plan applies to a specific driving situation (Kim et al., 2020).

This last proposal calls for a *rule-based system*, at least at the decision-making level, rather than a learning mechanism. Admittedly, rule-based AI became quite passé when deep learning entered the scene; it is often described as "good old-fashioned AI." Yet it has advantages beyond its ability to represent ethical action plans. One is *transparency*. If a car behaves inappropriately in some situation, engineers can trace the behavior directly to the action plan that causes it, and that action plan can be revised as necessary. A related advantage is *reasons-responsiveness*. If someone asks why the car took a certain turn, the system can give the reason, namely the if-part of the action plan it applied. One may question whether rule-based AI can execute highly complex tasks, but it is increasingly viewed as technically viable and even necessary due to the non-transparency of deep learning. Regarding autonomous cars, Brandom (2018) states, "Many companies have shifted to rule-based AI, an older technique that lets engineers hard-code specific behaviors or logic into an otherwise self-directed system." An enormous number of rules may be necessary, but the technical community has ample experience at accurately coding and debugging huge rule-based systems. An ordinary (non-self-driving) automobile is already regulated by more than 100,000 lines of code. The current trend in AI may therefore mesh well with ethical principles.

Online privacy

Privacy is an ancient concern of humankind, but invasive technology has a way of raising this concern anew. The advent of photojournalism in the late nineteenth century stoked fears of prying reporters who might publish embarrassing snapshots in the newspaper. This worry may seem quaint in our era of constant electronic surveillance, but it helped to inspire the first modern analysis of privacy rights in a seminal article by Samuel Warren and future U.S. Supreme Court justice Louis Brandeis (1890). Philosophers have followed up with much discussion of privacy rights, but without reaching consensus, even as the need for consensus becomes increasingly intense.

Surveillance today is more pervasive than often realized. Internet service providers record every website we visit, while some of those websites record our every keystroke. Smart phones track our location, ubiquitous cameras peer at us and identify our faces, and voice recognition software eavesdrops on our conversations at home. Retailers record every purchase and monitor our movements as we shop. License plate readers and parking meters track our cars, and smart televisions register what we are watching (perhaps while watching *us*). Sophisticated data mining algorithms prowl social networks and data bases to connect the dots and assemble dossiers for practically everyone who is online. The collected information is exchanged, bought, and sold round the clock at light speed, except where this is prohibited by law, and perhaps even there. While governments are voracious data consumers, often for nefarious ends, business organizations are major players as well, and they are often contracted by governments to carry out surveillance or provide the technology for doing so. Indeed, business and government are often locked in battle over who will control and have access to personal data.

Much of the privacy debate centers on whether there is an irreducible "right" to privacy and whether there should be legal protections (Warren and Brandeis, 1890; Thomson, 1975; Scanlon, 1975; Parent, 1983; Nissenbaum, 2010; Allen, 2011; Rössler, 2015). We steer clear of both issues. As always, we proceed by applying ethical principles directly to the business person's dilemma rather than attempting an analysis of right claims or public policy. We want to know whether a company can ethically collect personal data online and/or share it with others.

Turning first to the generalization principle, the most obvious ethical problem is that customers may be deceived about what happens to their personal information, and deception merely for profit is not generalizable. There is ample opportunity to be misled, especially since many people continue to be somewhat naïve about how companies exploit their data. Facebook and other social media platforms tout "privacy settings," which suggest that proper settings can limit access to private data. In reality, they only limit access by other users, while the company collects all the data it wants. Websites routinely provide a "privacy notice" that begins, "We care about your privacy." However, if one carefully reads through many paragraphs of fine print, one typically finds that the company reserves the right to collect and share all the data it wants. A company that wishes to avoid deception need only alert customers that any information they provide online will be collected, recorded, and shared with advertisers. It should also warn customers that they may unknowingly provide data through their Internet Protocol (IP) address, operating system characteristics, third-party cookies, browsing history, embedded tracking pixels, and super cookies (which are almost impossible to delete). The IP address and operating system may seem innocuous details, but they are sufficiently distinctive of a particular user to be helpful in deducing one's identity. Unfortunately, this kind of honesty on a website is extremely rare.

A deeper problem with generalizability emerges when one considers the cultural role of privacy. It has often been remarked that privacy is necessary for intimacy (Gerstein, 1978; Inness, 1992; Cohen, 2002). While observers from individualistic Western cultures tend to focus on the importance of intimacy for self-realization, it may also serve the universal purpose of making the family possible. Pair bonding and child raising require access to the most private information about those involved. Much of this information must remain private if it is not to be exploited by unfriendly forces. Intimacy and trust within the family are therefore essential to society, which could not long survive if invasion of privacy were general practice. Electronic surveillance that pries into one's most private affairs may therefore be ungeneralizable and unethical, since almost any purpose it might have would be undermined by social breakdown.

It may appear that privacy is not really essential to society, in view of the fact that different cultures have very different privacy norms. In fact, traditional peoples sometimes live in close quarters with other families and seem to have no privacy at all. Yet anthropologists tell us that every culture values privacy in some form (Altman, 1977). This includes traditional peoples, who may take care not to intrude on another family's space in a common dwelling, and who may erect partitions at times like childbirth. They may even lie to each other in order to conceal private matters. Perhaps the common thread across cultures is that they insist on privacy when its invasion undermines an essential social practice. If so, sufficiently intrusive electronic surveillance is ungeneralizable and unethical, although what counts as an unethical intrusion depends on the cultural context. In much of Europe, for example, we see a concern with privacy of information, as evidenced by the European Union's General Data Protection Regulation. The sanctity of the home is particularly important in the Middle East, while privacy of intimate relationships is paramount in Confucian cultures. To achieve generalizability, a company must understand and respect the role of privacy in the cultures where it operates.

A utilitarian assessment of data harvesting is inconclusive. While its widespread use can have the deleterious effects just described, what matters for the utilitarian principle is the impact of a given company's activity. It is often argued that commercial surveillance is as harmless as it is ubiquitous. It actually has some positive benefits, as it allows companies to target advertisements precisely, thus furthering the goal of matching supply and demand that is the root mission of marketing. Yet there is a risk of harm as well. The recording and sharing of sensitive data places this information on multiple repositories, some less secure than others. This dangles an irresistible temptation before hackers who profit from selling data. By one reckoning, there were over 1500 data breaches in the U.S. in 2019, exposing some 165 million sensitive records (Clement, 2020). It has become an almost daily occurrence, leading to "data breach fatigue" and quasi-acceptance of the phenomenon. Yet it incurs an enormous cost to consumers who are hit with identity theft and fraudulent charges, as well as banks and other companies that must clean up the mess while dealing with lawsuits and irate customers. While a given company or consumer may be lucky enough to have no problems, it is the expected cost that matters for the utilitarian assessment, taking into account the probabilities. There are ways to mitigate the risk of a breach significantly, and it seems clear that many companies are lax about security, perhaps due to the up-front aggravation and cost. To comply with the utilitarian principle, a company must take all reasonable steps to protect sensitive data, and share it only with trusted organizations (if any). This can be viewed as insurance against a devastating breach. Given this level of effort, the collection and sharing of personal data could be utilitarian on balance, but the issue deserves more careful study.

The autonomy principle is the hardest to apply to the privacy issue, but perhaps the decisive one over the long term. Several writers have remarked a connection between privacy and autonomy (Kupfer, 1987; Reiman, 2004; Moore, 2010; Allen, 2011; Francis and Francis, 2017), although they understand autonomy in different senses, including psychological self-realization of some kind. The question before us is whether privacy invasion violates moral autonomy by interfering with ethical action plans. Collection of intimate data does not, in and of itself, imply autonomy violation in this sense, although it could of course lead to this if the information falls into the wrong hands. Yet one might argue that surveillance alone could compromise autonomy if it were sufficiently pervasive. One can imagine a science-fiction world in which our minds are constantly open to scrutiny by strangers. We would be self-conscious about every thought. We could perhaps become objects manipulated by others, even if they exert no direct control, rather than autonomous beings. Jeremy Bentham, who was ahead of his time in so many ways, envisioned a similar possibility in the eighteenth century with his famous idea of a Panopticon. This was to be a prison or other institution in which a single supervisor could secretly observe any inmate at any time, creating the experience of being under constant surveillance. Bentham (1787, p. 31) described this as "a new mode of obtaining power of mind over mind." One might argue that our age of surveillance has already constructed an electronic Panopticon (Reiman, 2004), at least for those who live much of their lives online, as many do. As online connectivity increasingly saturates our consciousness, we may not be far from true loss of autonomy.

These reflections suggest that while electronic data harvesting by business is not necessarily unethical, if carried out responsibly, it is problematic. It can slip into conduct that is deceptive, harmful, socially dysfunctional, or incompatible with human autonomy. It must be carefully watched.

Technological unemployment

The AI revolution could lead to mass unemployment that has not been seen in history. There is no consensus on whether this threat is real in the long term, as many say that the AI-based economy will create new jobs, as did the first Industrial Revolution. Yet current trends are ominous. AI has already taken over much of manufacturing, and it is not uncommon for a factory floor to be devoid of human beings. Warehousing and retailing are shedding workers by the day, and the automation of freight transport and delivery is just around the corner. AI-based systems are encroaching on white-collar services, such as credit rating, investment advice, online advertisement placement, college admissions, job applicant screening, customer relations (through chatbots), and most controversially, parole decisions (O'Neil, 2017). Robots are replacing aides in some nursing homes and home care roles, and machines are overtaking medical technicians and even doctors in their ability to read and interpret scans.

Business organizations find themselves at the mercy of these larger forces, but their decisions can nonetheless contribute to technological unemployment. It is their choice whether to replace their blue-collar workers with robots, or white-collar workers with software. The generalization and utilitarian principles are most relevant to whether these choices are ethical.

One might argue that keeping up with technology is obligatory, even when it displaces workers, because a failure to do so is ungeneralizable. The main rationale for resisting technology is presumably to avoid layoffs that force workers into unemployment or low-paying jobs. Yet the ability of the firm to provide good-paying jobs even now is contingent on the fact that business managers have historically adopted new technology, even when doing so made workers redundant. The generalization principle is trans-temporal: it requires that the reasons for an action be consistent with generalization in the past as well as the future. Resisting new technology to save jobs therefore appears to be ungeneralizable. This argument has some merit, but it relies on a factual assumption that past managers could have created technological progress only by laying off their own workers. While their innovations might inevitably have caused layoffs at other firms, the claim in question is that one should displace workers at one's own firm, if necessary, in order to adopt new technology. If today's good-paying jobs could have resulted from a history in which technology *adopters* never laid off workers (or laid off only a few workers while hiring many more), then a refusal to dismiss workers today is generalizable. A glance into the past reveals that entrepreneurs who adopted path-breaking technology often built new businesses that created jobs rather than laying off existing employees. One thinks of Isambard Brunel, Ernest Solvay, Henry Ford, George Westinghouse,[1] and many others, up to Steve Jobs and Elon Musk of recent times, all of whom followed this pattern. It is unclear that a manager is rationally constrained to reject

---

[1]   During his early career, George Westinghouse lived in a modest residence that still stands around the corner from my house in Pittsburgh. He changed the world by introducing the AC-powered electric grid (with technical help from Nikola Tesla) and inventions that make rail transport practical to this day. In the process, he earned the enduring admiration of his employees for progressive labor relations. He later built a model town for employees (Wilmerding, PA) that is reminiscent of the utopian community of New Lanark, Scotland. The nearby Westinghouse Electric Works and his Union Switch and Signal plant, both adjoining Pittsburgh, provided more than 10,000 good-paying jobs.

this interpretation of history, and if so we have no compelling case for an obligation to adopt technology by displacing workers.

A utilitarian assessment of technology adoption depends on how its benefits are distributed as well as their aggregate utility (Chapter 3), and distribution is a complicated matter. A company that relies on AI rather than human workers undoubtedly contributes to labor productivity, which is good in principle because it increases wealth per capita without increasing how much people must work for it. Yet when fewer workers are involved in the creation of wealth, it becomes harder to spread it around. We already see a concentration of productive capacity in today's man-ufacturing sector, where relatively few workers are employed due to its extraordinary efficiency. This surplus is distributed, however imperfectly, through several mechanisms that include government welfare programs but rely to a great extent on the structure of the economy itself. The very fact that manufactured goods are cheap allows consumers to share in the surplus, and many people earn a living through the design, distribution, sale, operation, and repair of manufactured goods. Organized labor has also played a key distributive role, even if it has weakened considerably in the Anglo-American sphere. The resulting increase in disposable income is passed along to a large professional class, a financial sector that controls credit, and other companies and individuals that collect economic rent in various ways. Yet as AI technology concentrates value creation in an ever smaller segment of the population, there is no assurance that these mechanisms, which already permit growing wealth inequality, can be expanded to meet the challenge. Various government responses have been proposed, such as a universal basic income, advocated even by doc-trinaire libertarians F. A. Hayek (1960) and Milton Friedman (1962), and a universal capital inheritance, sometimes called a "capital homestead" in reference to a historical land-grant program in the U.S. It is unclear, however, that the political will for such programs will ever exist. It is still less clear how the economy can be restructured to support a large popu-lation that lacks paid employment through no fault of their own (Hooker and Kim, 2019).

It is against this confusing backdrop that a company must decide whether to move into AI technology. Consider, for example, a ridesharing and delivery service like Uber or Lyft. By adopting autonomous cars and drones, the company potentially creates utility on several fronts. It cuts costs by removing the expense and management of human drivers, making the company more efficient. It boosts labor productivity by providing transportation and delivery with fewer workers involved. It avoids road accidents by replacing delivery vehicles with drones and human drivers with machines. Yet it deprives thousands of drivers of income in an economy that increasingly relies on contingent labor, with the concomitant disruption to their lives and families. It transfers wealth from these drivers to executives and stockholders, exacerbating inequality. Research and development efforts that enable this strategy[2] are likewise fraught with ambivalence. By accelerating the introduction of autonomous control, they may substantially reduce death and injury in road accidents. At the same time, they help to destroy the livelihood of millions of taxi and truck drivers, which will no doubt heighten political instability and polarization. A futility argument probably does not apply in this context. The company cannot argue that if it does not adopt autonomous control, some other company will, because its unique position may allow it to hasten the development of AI in ways that other companies cannot. This creates costs and benefits that would not otherwise exist, at least in the short term.

A company contemplating adoption of AI is faced with one of four possible scenarios. First, the company may be forced to rely on AI to survive in a competitive market, in which case it is better to do so than suffer the unmitigated evil of being driven out of business. Second, the company may be able to adopt AI without reducing staff, or by reducing staff through attrition, which substantially reduces the downside of using AI. A third and related possibility is that the company may be able to retain staff by allowing them to combine forces with AI, in a strategy known as *augmentation*. Suggested decades ago by Englebart (1962), augmentation moves beyond automation by using machines to enhance human capabilities rather than displace them. As noted in Chapter 6, allowing humans to work alongside robots, train them, and help design the systems in which they operate can create a win–win situation. It not only saves good-paying jobs but boosts company productivity by joining human creativity with machine reliability. At the same time, it enhances the capability, motivation, and dignity of workers by giving them an active and meaningful role in the company (Davenport and Kirby, 2015; Hooker and Kim, 2019). Yet one must take care to design robotic co-workers ("cobots") without gra-

---

[2]   Uber currently funds a major autonomous vehicle research project at Carnegie Mellon University, where I am employed.

tuitous humanlike qualities, which could encourage workers to anthropomorphize them in unhealthy ways (Kwon et al., 2016; Christakis, 2019; Hooker and Kim, 2020).

In the fourth scenario, none of these possibilities are present. The company can only make its best educated guess as to the consequences of adopting new technology, taking into account the social factors outlined here. The utilitarian principle requires nothing more.

8 Cross-cultural business ethics

An ethical principle for working across cultures

The ethical analysis conducted in previous chapters is rooted in the Western tradition and may seem unsuited to provide guidance for working across cultures. Yet Western and most other cultural traditions have resources for regulating cross-cultural business. Archaeological evidence shows that trade between different peoples has been carried out successfully for eons. A Western approach can be discerned by returning to the fundamental task of ethics: to build rational consensus on how people can live and work together. This leads to a generalization principle that asks us to act according to policies that can be generally adopted without undermining the practices and institutions that make it possible to achieve the purposes of the actions. One need only transfer this rule to another cultural context to obtain the following special case of the generalization principle:

Generalization principle for cross-cultural business: A business policy undertaken in another culture is ethical only if one can rationally believe that the policy could be generally adopted without undermining the cultural practices and institutions that make it possible to achieve the purposes of the policy.

This does not simply mean that when in Rome, one should do as the Romans do. A business is required to conform to local business practices only when those practices are necessary to allow the system to work, because a business cannot achieve its purposes unless the system works. For example, there is no need to engage in bribery and kickbacks even when they are widespread. They tend to undermine rather than support cultural institutions, just as widespread practices in Western countries are sometimes dysfunctional. On the other hand, such practices as gift giving and cronyism that are often unethical in the West may satisfy the principle, because they are integral to the business system when done properly. A major goal of this chapter is to indicate, at least in outline, how one might distinguish local practices that support the system from those that tend to undermine it.

One might object that an entire system might be unethical by Western standards, even if it works quite well on its own terms and allows foreign businesses to operate successfully. The generalization principle just stated is, in fact, only a necessary condition, not a sufficient condition, for ethical conduct. Even in a Western context, actions that satisfy the generalization principle may be unethical on other grounds, perhaps because they violate the utilitarian or autonomy principle. A fuller analysis of cross-cultural ethics requires deeper insights and cultural knowledge than can be developed in this short book. Yet the above generalization principle can be a useful guide as a necessary condition. One knows at least to avoid business activities that, if generalized, would tend to undermine local institutions that make business possible.

Since ethical action requires some understanding of how a cultural system works, it is necessary to begin with an attempt to describe and classify different cultural systems, at least at a high level. The chapter then proceeds to illustrate these concepts with brief international case studies involving possible corruption, and how one might deal with these situations. This is followed by two case studies involving international supply chains. Throughout this discussion, *no attempt is made to judge which cultures are "better."* Every culture has a logic of its own, as it has developed norms and ethical sensibilities that allow it to function successfully. Every culture finds somewhat different solutions to life's problems, and it can be useful and enlightening to learn how they do it. Indeed, cultures have borrowed ideas from each other for millennia, a practice that is today more vital than ever in a crowded and complicated world that is increasingly difficult to manage.

How cultures differ

It is often said that modern transportation and communications are moving the world toward cultural homogeneity. If this is true, cross-cultural understanding is becoming steadily less important. Yet internationally experienced business people know that the cultural situation on the ground varies enormously. Even subcultures within a single country may require different approaches to business. While travel is easier and cheaper than ever, only a lucky few experience international travel. The vast majority of people who do the actual work in most countries have never traveled abroad and grow up in a culture with strong local characteristics. As for communication technologies, electronic media and social networking platforms are notorious for isolating people in a cultural bubble, the precise opposite of homogenization.

There are some 5000 cultures in the world, many of them radically different in their basic assumptions and approach to life. The subtleties and fascinations of any one country could fill many books, and the present discussion can only offer an overview of basic concepts. Before interacting with people from an unfamiliar country, readers are encouraged to study that country in depth, perhaps using the framework presented here to organize their thoughts. I develop the framework in greater detail elsewhere (Hooker, 2003, 2009, 2012).

We begin with a very broad distinction that is nonetheless useful in practice: relationship-based versus rule-based cultures. In *relationship-based* cultures, life is organized primarily around personal relationships and the loyalties they require. They are found in most of the world, including Asia, Africa, Latin America, and to some extent in parts of Europe. In *rule-based* cultures, life is regulated primarily by rules that have authority in their own right. These cultures occur in regions that are cultural offspring of Europe, including Australia, Canada, New Zealand, the U.S., and of course Europe itself. We hasten to add that no country is purely relationship-based or rule-based, and in fact neither mechanism could operate successfully in isolation. Yet one or the other is typically dominant. The concept of *yīn-yáng* in ancient Chinese philosophy captures the idea: for any pair of opposites, either is leavened by a little of the other.

Relationship-based cultures are characterized by several practices. Perhaps most important to business is the primacy of relationship building over deal making. Business in the West is primarily about deals: negotiating the deal, formalizing the deal in a contract, executing the terms of the deal, and perhaps bringing a lawsuit if one party reneges on the deal. Business in the rest of the world is primarily about building business relationships. Rather than reliance on a formally negotiated deal, there is a mutual understanding as to how the business partners will collaborate. The contract (if any) has at most secondary importance, although it can be essential in some areas, such as parts of the Middle East. The mutual understanding evolves as the situation changes from day to day, with no need to renegotiate a contract. Rather than rely on law courts to enforce a deal, business partners build a trust relationship, perhaps over a period of years.

Relationships play an equally important role in the everyday process of getting things done. One normally works through personal connections (or through an intermediary such as a *wasta* in the Middle East or *despachante* in Brazil) to secure a permit, license, visa, job, or even a visit to the doctor. This is of course true to some extent everywhere. Yet while it is sometimes possible in Western countries to obtain a white-collar job solely on the basis of one's résumé, this is well-nigh unthinkable in much of the world, where a personal contact is necessary. People likewise manage stress through relationships. When there are problems, one relies on the extended family and friends for support, rather than professionals or the legal system. Even vehicular traffic reveals the cultural contrast. It may appear chaotic, but drivers successfully move through an intersection or enter a main thoroughfare by one-on-one negotiation with other drivers, rather than following traffic laws that may require one to wait for a signal or a gap in the traffic.

Rules lie at the heart of the relationship-based/rule-based distinction. Both types of society may have many rules and laws, but the difference stems from the source of authority. A relationship-based society invests authority in certain persons, and the rules are binding only when they are laid down by people in authority. One owes obedience to persons with whom one has a certain kind of relationship: perhaps one's parents, grandparents, boss, or head of state—and yes, sometimes one's husband.

In rule-based societies, people with authority obtain that authority from the rules. Even the head of state must (at least theoretically) come to power as specified in a legal rulebook, rather than by virtue of one's wealth, connections with important families, or influence over the military. While it is not hard to understand how authority in relationship-based cultures derives from pre-existing dependency relationships, such as parent and child, one may ask how mere rules can acquire authority in Western countries. The rules must be seen as *inherently logical and reasonable*, so that people comply voluntarily (Chapter 1). While laws are often regarded as legitimate when enacted by majority vote, this is only because a policy of majority rule is seen as itself reasonable. It is this need for rational consensus that underlies the ethical analysis presented in this book.

Authority is closely related to ethics, because authority can maintain social order only if it is supported by ethics. Differences in the source of authority give rise to different ethical norms. In relationship-based cultures, ethics centers around respect and care. Respect for authority is necessary to preserve order, and care is necessary to maintain relationships that are the basis for that authority. The highest obligation, aside from obedience, is to promote the welfare of those that participate in these relationships, such as one's extended family or perhaps one's superiors and subordinates. In rule-based cultures, adherence to self-justifying rules is the basis of social order. Ethics centers around equality and fairness, because everyone is subject to the same rules, which are seen as universally binding because they are rooted in logic. Everyone is therefore equal in some sense. Any person who exercises rational choice is an autonomous individual, and one's highest obligation is to respect the autonomy of others.

Classification of cultures

A number of schemes for classifying cultures have been developed, primarily by Edward T. Hall (1959, 1966, 1983) and Geert Hofstede (1980; Hofstede et al., 2010; House et al., 2004, 2014). Three classifications are particularly relevant to business ethics, and we summarize them here. They correlate with relationship-based and rule-based systems: relationship-based cultures exhibit high power distance, are shame-based, and rely on high-context communication, while rule-based cultures exhibit low power distance, are guilt-based, and rely on low-context communication. These and other classifications never tell the full story about a culture, but they provide a vocabulary and framework that can call attention to cultural mechanisms and help to describe them.

Power distance is the degree to which less powerful people accept their subordinate position. High power distance characterizes relationship-based cultures, because they rely on individuals with inherent authority to maintain order. In business, the boss is expected to take charge and make decisions unilaterally, subject to instructions from his own superiors. Employees are reluctant to challenge the boss or discuss problems in the company, at least in front of others, because this causes loss of face and perhaps loss of respect that is necessary for authority. However, a good boss is expected to take care of employees, and his authority is partially legitimated by his ability to do so. The boss makes decisions regarding an employee's time off and the like on a case-by-case basis, taking into account the employee's personal situation. In Confucian cultures, the boss is often regarded as a father figure who may give advice to subordinates about life in general. There are similar expectations from a political leader. An example might be China's Deng Xiaoping, who was authoritarian (he supported the infamous 1989 crackdown on protests in Tiānānmén Square) but acted on behalf of his people by laying the foundation for extraordinary economic growth.

Low power distance is characteristic of rule-based cultures. The ideal boss exercises consultative management and is expected to defend decisions on a rational basis. Employees regularly bring concerns and grievances to the boss. A good boss is not so much expected to take care of employees as to inspire them and treat them equally. Regarding personnel decisions like time off, bosses generally prefer to go by the book rather than make case-by-case decisions. After rotating out of office, a boss or political leader becomes an ordinary citizen with no inherent authority, at least in theory.

Shame-based and *guilt-based* cultures rely on different psychological mechanisms for enforcing behavior norms. The two can occur together, but one or the other normally dominates. A person experiences shame when others become aware of inappropriate behavior and call it out, while guilt is a private feeling that one can experience when no one is aware of the bad behavior ("guilt" can also refer to culpability for an act, but we use the psychological sense here). Shame is dominant in relationship-based cultures and can take the form of loss of face, embarrassment, humiliation, or public punishment. The role of shame in these cultures leads to a vitally important management principle of which Westerners are too seldom aware: a good boss is expected to provide direct and constant supervision of employees, to make sure inappropriate behavior is observed. In fact, a failure to monitor compliance with a company policy can be taken as permission to violate it. This does not mean that employees are unethical, but only reflects an assumption that an unenforced rule is not really important. The mobile phone achieved instant popularity in shame-based cultures when it was introduced, partly because it is an ideal means for the boss to keep tab on subordinates even while he is away from the office. In rule-based cultures, employees tend to feel guilty about inadequate performance or violation of company rules. The feeling is of course reinforced by a fear of being caught at some point, but supervision nonetheless tends to be light, and employees may resent someone looking over their shoulder.

High-context and *low-context* cultures manage information in different ways. In high-context cultures, information and norms are absorbed from the social context, while in low-context cultures, they are explicitly written down. An immediate clue that one is entering a low-context country is that information and rules are posted everywhere. It is difficult to overestimate the importance of this distinction for business. In low-context cultures, employees are expected to pay attention to written rules and make themselves aware of company policy. Someone who wants to take a week off will consult the company vacation policy, perhaps posted online, before speaking to the boss about it. In a high-context culture, employees are likely to ignore posted policies, company memos, or signs on the wall. They expect to be personally apprised of the rules by an immediate superior. This is obviously consistent with the preference for personal supervision implied by high power distance.

Low-context communication supports the central role of the written contract in rule-based cultures. A long, dense, Western-style contract can be a source of bewilderment or even disgust for business people elsewhere, due to its penchant for spelling out every conceivable contingency. Due to its thoroughness, the contract is the governing force in any Western business undertaking. No commitment is taken seriously unless it is in the contract. By contrast, in a high-context culture, *no commitment is taken seriously unless it is part of the relationship.* Simply writing something into the contract has little meaning. A failure to realize this key difference is probably the chief cause of failure and disappointment in cross-cultural business.

Corruption

Business people tend to encounter differences in ethical norms most obviously when dealing with corruption. One can define corruption as activity that *corrupts*; that is, as activity that, if widely practiced, tends to undermine a cultural system. The obligation to avoid corruption stems directly from the generalization principle stated at the beginning of the chapter. Precisely because a universal practice of corrupt behavior would, by definition, undermine the cultural institutions that make business possible, it is not generalizable. Different business systems work differently and are therefore corrupted in different ways, making it vital to recognize what types of activities are corrupting in a given country.

Western observers tend to identify corruption with behavior that is more prevalent elsewhere, such as bribery, ignoring the fact that corruption is an equal threat at home but takes a different form. Every culture has a different set of weaknesses that make it susceptible to a particular type of corruption. Bribery may occur in relationship-based cultures because it is a shortcut to the arduous task of building the long-term relationships that are so essential to business. Cheating of various kinds can occur in rule-based countries that are characterized by light supervision, where relationships are less important and one can get away with cheating more easily.

We present here several case studies of conduct that may or may not be corrupting and indicate how to assess the situation. All of the case studies describe real events. None of these examples are intended to suggest that some countries are more corrupt than others. On the contrary, *corruption occurs everywhere.* The examples only illustrate how it takes different forms in different cultural systems.

Side payments versus *guānxì*

An experienced international businessman, whom we will call Mr. L, was assigned by a well-known U.S. company to a branch office in Taipei, Taiwan. On one occasion he met with a team representing a potential Taiwanese supplier. When the team departed, he noticed that one of them left his briefcase behind. Mr. L opened the briefcase to identify the owner and found it stuffed with cash. He immediately surmised that he had been offered a *kickback*. The Taiwanese team was offering to "kick back" to Mr. L some of the profits that their firm would earn if he awarded them a contract. Some euphemistically refer to this type of payment as a "commission," which is incorrect. A commission is a payment one receives from one's own company as a reward for bringing in business, while a kickback comes from another company that is seeking business. As it happened, Mr. L's company explicitly forbids accepting kickbacks in its Code of Conduct. Since Mr. L could carry out his business without accepting this type of bribe, it was an easy decision to reject the kickback. He dispatched a trusted employee to return the briefcase to the owner. He then sent a vaguely worded email to the team's boss that he was returning the "lost property" he found in his office. This was to ensure that the boss knew that the bribe money had not been delivered, since otherwise the briefcase owner might keep it.

While Mr. L's decision was relatively easy in this case, in other cases he might have been expected to supply a kickback before business could proceed. So it is important to understand whether kickbacks are in fact corrupting in this cultural environment. They are. Business in Chinese culture has long relied on a type of personal relationship known as *guānxì*, which is Mandarin Chinese for relationship or connection. *Guānxì* partners build mutual trust over a period of years by doing favors for each other. They deal with each other in good faith, because they want to maintain their relationship in a business environment where *guānxì* is highly valued. *Guānxì* provides the stability and predictability that is necessary for advanced civilization, much as contracts do in the West. If one is constructing a Three Gorges Dam, it is imperative to know that cement shipments will arrive when needed three years down the road, and *guānxì* ensures this. Because it takes patience and persistence to develop *guānxì*, there is an ever present temptation to take a shortcut by building a relationship on side payments rather than trust. Yet as John D. Rockefeller once remarked, you can buy people, but they don't stay bought. Kickbacks and other bribes do not provide the stability civilization requires, and if generalized, they would undermine the prosperous Taiwanese economy that makes Mr. L's business possible. This is why kickbacks are corrupting and ungeneralizable in Taiwan.

The ethical assessment would be different if Mr. L had awarded the contract to a trusted Taiwanese partner, even though the partner's bid were less attractive on paper than some other bids. This is generalizable because it is an exercise of *guānxì*. True, it would be regarded as a conflict of interest in a low-context Western setting, because Mr. L's interest in doing business with friends would conflict with the company's interest in awarding contracts based on transparently superior bids. Yet in a Confucian setting, there is no conflict of interest, because it is in the company's interest that Mr. L do business with a *guānxì* partner whose personal reliability outweighs any promises that might appear in writing. Favoring a *guānxì* partner in this way is often described pejoratively as *cronyism*, but it is responsible cronyism. Cronyism becomes irresponsible and corrupting when one delivers favors to friends simply because they are friends, and not because the friendship connection is good for the company.

There are also legal considerations. To understand them, it is essential to distinguish bribes from extortion payments. A *bribe* is a payment that is intended to influence someone's judgment, when that judgment should be based on other factors. A kickback is clearly a bribe, because it is intended to influence a business judgment that should be based on price and quality. *Extortion* is the practice of demanding payments in exchange for something to which one is already entitled. For example, demanding payment for a business permit, when one has met the legal requirements for the permit, is extortion. *Facilitating payments*, sometimes called "grease payments," are small, routine extortion payments, as when an official demands payment for a driver's license, visa, or timely customs clearance for which one is already qualified.

As a U.S. national, Mr. L is subject to the 1977 Foreign Corrupt Practices Act, which forbids paying bribes in foreign countries only when they are paid to government officials. It does not prohibit extortion payments, bribes paid to business people, or facilitating payments. Mr. L could therefore pay kickbacks in Taiwan without violating this law. It would be otherwise if he were a British subject, because kickbacks violate the 2011

U.K. Bribery Act, which generally prohibits paying and receiving bribes of any kind in a foreign country. Various kinds of side payments may or may not be prohibited by local laws, and these laws may be strictly enforced or mere formalities that are universally ignored. Any firm that does business internationally is strongly advised to retain a respected international law firm, of which there are many, and managers should consult an attorney whenever a side payment is contemplated. They should bear in mind that, if one is arrested for violation of local laws, there is little one's national embassy can do.

Corruption in the finance industry

The financial crisis of 2008 provides a textbook example of corruption Western-style. It resulted from the ease with which firms could violate laws and professional standards in a cultural environment of weak supervision. The crisis began with a proliferation of subprime mortgage loans in the U.S. This alone is not an ethical problem, because properly vetted subprime loans can allow people with financial problems to borrow money and rehabilitate their credit rating, in exchange for a somewhat higher interest rate. But it coincided with the novel practice of immediately selling mortgage loans to big banks that package them in mortgage-backed securities. Mortgage lenders knew that someone else would be responsible for these high-risk loans and therefore failed to perform due diligence when evaluating borrowers, some of whom clearly lacked income to repay the loans. Worse, these complex securities contained "tranches" of loans with different risk levels, and even experienced buyers had difficulty evaluating them. Compounding the problem was the fact that ratings agencies such as Moody's, Fitch, and Standard & Poor's gave the securities AAA ratings despite the risky loans buried inside them. The banks pay these agencies to provide ratings, setting up an obvious conflict of interest, because an agency that provides substandard ratings may lose business to a more accommodating firm. As if this were not enough, the banks issuing the securities were already highly leveraged and operating at unacceptable risk levels in pursuit of ever higher returns. In addition, large insurers like AIG sold credit default swaps that ostensibly provided some kind of insurance against a drop in the value of the securities, but without nearly enough cash reserves to cover potential losses. The bubble burst, as bubbles always do, resulting in a credit freeze that crippled economies worldwide, and whose effects persist today. The U.S. government was obliged to provide a massive bailout of the financial system, triggering popular backlash and exacerbating political polarization that continues to threaten the country's democratic institutions.

At each stage of this debacle, professionals violated standards and laws that govern their industry, without immediate consequences. No one was looking. In fact, many who engaged in irresponsible behavior had already found new careers when the crisis hit. Legal prosecution was either non-existent or slow. The first legal action against a ratings agency, for example, did not begin until five years later (Viswanatha and LaCapra, 2013). This is an example of corruption as serious as any case of bribery one can name, or perhaps more serious. It clearly violates the generalization principle, because irresponsible behavior of this kind can, if generalized, bring down a financial system that relies on professional conduct. It very nearly did so.

Alleged bribery in India

The long saga of the Dabhol electric power plant began in 1992. Spearheaded by the infamous Texas-based firm Enron, it was India's largest ever private foreign investment up to that point. Bechtel and General Electric were also involved. Enron executives foresaw that India could become an information technology powerhouse in future years, particularly due to liberalization of the economy after the 1991 collapse of the Soviet Union. Yet an information economy needs reliable electric power, and the Indian power grid was not delivering it. Enron wanted to get in on the ground floor of power development. The trouble began when the Indian state of Maharashtra guaranteed Enron an eyebrow-raising 25 percent return on investment for the project. This was despite a projected high cost of electricity from the plant, due in part to Enron's intention to source expensive high-quality fuel (liquefied natural gas) from a facility in Qatar in which it owned part interest. There was widespread suspicion that Enron had bribed the state to guarantee a generous return on investment (Munde, 1995). This fed into the political situation of the day, because the upstart Hindu nationalist Bharatiya Janata Party (BJP) was challenging the long-ruling Congress Party over alleged corruption. The Indian government backed away from the Enron deal when the BJP took power in 1998 under Prime Minister A. B. Vajpayee. Alarmed, Enron CEO Ken Lay appealed to his friend in the White House, George Bush, who dispatched Vice President Dick Cheney and Secretary of State Colin Powell to India. Vajpayee refused to restore the agreement, as the BJP had stood for election on an anti-corruption platform. The ill-fated project was abandoned when Enron collapsed in 2001 due to a major business scandal in the U.S. The partially finished plant gathered rust until 2006, when two state-owned domestic companies took over the project. The plant resumed operation in 2010, producing power at a loss. Nine years later, India's Supreme Court finally closed the legal case regarding state corruption, with no clear resolution (Press Trust of India, 2019).

Without concluding whether bribery actually occurred, we can ask if it would have been corrupting in the Indian cultural environment. India is a mind-bogglingly complex pastiche of some 2000 ethnic groups. It has a strongly relationship-based heritage that mingles with Western elements dating from the British colonial period. Despite the complexity, one can observe that bribery is inconsistent with both the relationship-based and rule-based components of Indian society. The relationship-based side relies on durable social networks consisting of family and friendship connections. They are the key to getting anything done and the basis for stability in times of political upheaval, such as during the Ayodhya riots that took place as Enron was beginning its Indian venture. A foreign company should operate through these networks, perhaps beginning with Indian expats in its employ, to secure government and financial support. Sufficiently widespread bribery would undercut a networking mechanism that has sustained India for centuries (facilitating payments, quite common in India, are another matter). At the same time, bribery tends to undermine the rule-based elements of Indian society, including its democratic institutions and sophisticated legal system. Any attempt at bribery on Enron's part, assuming it occurred, reveals a serious misunderstanding of Indian culture as well as committing a double-edged violation of the generalization principle.

Nepotism in China

Lee Kum Kee (LKK) is a Chinese food and health products company that illustrates how nepotism can be functional in the right context. Founded in 1888 in rural Guangdong province, the Hong-Kong-based company is today an international enterprise that markets its products in over 100 countries. British readers may know it as the company that purchased London's "walkie-talkie" skyscraper in 2017, at a price that broke United Kingdom records for a building acquisition. It has been a family-owned company from the start. In the 1980s, the CEO and founder's grandson

Lee Man Tat sent his four sons to study in the U.S. (Lief and Ward, 2008). As they graduated, he asked them to return to China and work for the company. Motivated by obligation to their father (known as *filial piety* in a Confucian context), all four sons returned and were installed as heads of the company's four divisions. This confirmed what company managers knew: there was a ceiling on how far non-family members could advance in the firm. It is a clear case of nepotism (the word derives from the Latin for "uncle"), which is the practice of favoring family members in hiring decisions and otherwise.

Westerners look askance at nepotism, often seeing it as giving unfair advantage to family members who may be less qualified than others. Yet in a Confucian context, it can have at least two advantages. One is that due to filial piety, the boss commands greater loyalty and obedience from family members than other employees, and they may consequently work harder for the firm. A second is that the boss knows intimately the strengths and weaknesses of family members and can assign them duties accordingly. There is no need to rely on a résumé or second-hand information. Mr. Lee obviously placed his sons well, as LKK has continued to show remarkable growth and success. Responsible nepotism therefore need not be corrupting and, in the right cultural context, can be a positive factor. Nepotism becomes irresponsible and corrupting when relatives are hired simply because they are relatives, and not because their family connection confers a unique advantage.

Since LKK is an international firm that employs Western managers, one might worry that Confucian nepotism can lead to morale problems. Mr. Lee's sons have evidently been sensitive to this possibility, perhaps due to their college experience in the U.S., and have compensated in other ways. The youngest son, for example, is making sure that the firm does not practice the close supervision that is normally characteristic of a relationship-based Chinese business. He states, "We don't want our staff to feel that our presence or direction of strategy is imposing…I'd like to think that we have been careful enough in hiring and training the right people and providing an overall idea of where we're going, and why, that we don't need to be standing over anyone's shoulder" (Lief and Ward, 2008, p. 7).

Wasta in the Middle East

The Australian construction firm Leighton Holdings, now CIMIC Ltd., was involved in a Middle Eastern bribery scandal that began in 2010 and led to a string of arrests over the following decade (McKenzie, 2020). We focus specifically on the role of *wasta* in this affair with the aim of illustrating when it is corrupt and when it is legitimate. The Arabic-derived word *wasta* refers to influence with important people, as well as to an intermediary who uses this influence to obtain favors for others. Our story concerns two *wastas* who worked on behalf of Leighton, and to whom we refer as Mr. A and Mr. B. In 2007, Leighton purchased a 45 percent stake in Al-Habtoor Engineering, a major Dubai construction firm, and engaged Mr. A as chairman of the joint venture Habtoor Leighton Group. Mr. A had contacts with influential families in the region and soon began to find business for Leighton, such as an Australian $515 million contract to build the Habtoor Palace Hotel (Australian Associated Press, 2012). A couple of years later, Leighton engaged Mr. B to round up projects in the Middle East and elsewhere. One of these projects was reportedly a $750 million oil pipeline in Iraq. According to a whistle blower, Mr. B received a 10 percent kickback on some of the projects and passed part of the cash to Leighton executives (McKenzie and Baker, 2013). At this point the scandal broke in the Australian media.

Though *wasta* is often identified with corruption in the Middle East, it can be entirely legitimate. Historically, a *wasta* was an intermediary between clans or tribes in the Arab world. In recent times, *wastas* use their connections with important people to obtain jobs, promotions, university admission, contracts, and government dispensations for those they assist. A trusted *wasta* can perform a valuable service to a busy decision maker by conveying worthy petitions, while screening out less deserving requests. A *wasta* of this kind does not collect kickbacks or other quid pro quo rewards, but benefits from the prestige he gains from his role. Mr. A was a totally legitimate *wasta* who, from all appearances, was directly compensated only by his salary. His activity supported a cultural system characterized by high power distance and was clearly generalizable. Mr. B, however, engaged in the kind of behavior that gives *wasta* a bad reputation. Because he was motivated by kickbacks, he had little credibility as a judicious intermediary. This type of *wasta* is corrupting because it hampers the ability of influential families to make informed decisions in a society where they are often the primary decision makers.

Avoiding bribery in sub-Saharan Africa

Mo Ibrahim and Terry Rhodes founded Celtel International[1] in 1998 with
the aim of bringing an affordable mobile telephone service to sub-Saharan
Africa (Mullins and Rhodes, 2011). Ibrahim is Sudanese and believed that
he understood the continent well enough to do business without slipping
into bribery. The company devised clever strategies for avoiding corruption and succeeded in several countries. On one occasion, however, it
hit a brick wall. Celtel had purchased a $750,000 operating license, but
final approval bogged down. Eager to get to the bottom of the problem,
Rhodes and CEO Alan Rudge arranged a meeting with government officials to discuss the matter. When the meeting commenced, there was an
awkward silence. The officials seemed to be expecting something. After
some pleasantries, the meeting concluded without any progress on the
license issue. Rhodes and Rudge later learned that their home office in
Amsterdam had received a fax from the government that morning. It
listed the officials who had agreed to attend the meeting, and next to each
name was a monetary amount, totaling some $50,000. The payments were
required in exchange for initiating the discussion, and further bribes may
be required later.

Bribery is indeed a frequent occurrence in sub-Saharan Africa, but it is
more a symptom than a cause of corruption. It stems from the breakdown of a traditional type of leadership that is somewhat akin to the "big
man" system first identified by anthropologists in Melanesia (Sahlins,
1963). A village chief earns popular support and thereby accumulates
wealth in exchange for sharing his wealth with those in need. It is a kind
of social welfare system that enhances the survivability of the village and
spreads throughout society for this reason. This tradition, combined with
a strongly collectivist culture, persists to this day in an expectation that
those who possess wealth and advantages will share them.[2] However, the
big man style of leadership began to collapse as European powers colo-
nized Africa after the abolition of chattel slavery. Colonial governments
were set up in central cities, and they became national governments fol-

---

[1] The company was founded as MSI Cellular Investments, renamed Celtel in
2004, acquired by Zain in 2005, and by Airtel in 2010, when it was renamed
Airtel.
[2] I experienced this in many ways while living among the Shona people in
Zimbabwe.

lowing decolonization. Village leaders migrated to the capital to assume government jobs, an environment in which they were no longer subject to the social pressure that had guided their behavior back home. A practice of obtaining influence by redistributing wealth evolved into a practice of gaining influence by paying off officials in the capital. Bribery is therefore one symptom of a wholesale corruption of social organization that stems from a clash of radically different cultures and world views.

This perspective suggests a possible strategy for circumventing bribery: substitute popular support for the bribes. This strategy lies at the root of some tactics that Celtel used successfully. On one occasion, the company avoided paying tribute to a chief by contributing to improvements in the local school. The chief forgot about collecting payments when he saw he could take credit for the improvements and earn favor with the community. One might call this a bribe, but it could equally well be regarded as the sort of infrastructure development that foreign companies often fund in developing economies. As such, it is generalizable. On another occasion, customs officials demanded extortion payments before they would release Celtel's equipment. The company dealt with this by organizing a big media event to announce the arrival of mobile phones, to which political dignitaries were invited. The prospect of getting phones generated the same frenzied excitement it incites worldwide, and the politicians were eager to harvest public gratitude by presiding over the introduction of these marvelous devices. Customs officials had no choice but to release the equipment.

Supply chain ethics

The world today is draped by a complex network of supply chains that deliver manufactured goods from low-wage to high-wage countries. Merchants on the receiving end sometimes find themselves in the embarrassing position of accepting shipments from factories with hazardous or exploitative working conditions. Yet they are unsure how they can influence conduct at the far end of a supply chain that may pass through a half-dozen firms. Because these chains span cultural boundaries, awareness of differences between relationship-based and rule-based cultures can provide a clue (Hooker, 2014). Two case studies illustrate how. One involves a toy manufacturing scandal in China, and the other dangerous working conditions in the South Asian garment industry.

A toy factory in China

Lee Der Industrial Company was a Chinese supplier of toys to Western companies. By 2007, it had shipped toys to Mattel and its subsidiary, Fisher-Price, for several years. Lee Der was run by Zhang Shuhong, who was so dedicated to the company that he slept in a small room at the factory. Unfortunately, Mattel discovered that the paint on the toys contained dangerous quantities of lead, and it recalled some 1 million toys. Following the scandal, the Chinese government rescinded Lee Der's operating license. Mr. Zhang regretfully called a meeting of his employees and told them they must find jobs elsewhere. Overcome with shame, he retreated into his back room and hung himself (Barboza, 2007).

The circumstances behind this tragic story were never fully described in the media (Kenney, 2007), but they teach a valuable cultural lesson. Mr. Zhang sourced paint from his trusted *guānxì* partner Liang Jiacheng at Dongxiong New Energy. Mr. Liang found himself short of pigment and decided to follow the trendy new practice of ordering it online. He obtained the pigment from people he did not know at Dongguan Zhongxin Toner Factory. They sent certificates of lead-free pigment along with the toner shipments, but the certificates were forged. Unknown to Mr. Liang, he ended up supplying lead-based paint to his good friend Mr. Zhang.

It is instructive to examine each link of this supply chain. The link between Mattel and Lee Der traversed the relationship-based/rule-based divide. Their contract contained a provision that required lead testing of all toys. Mattel, operating on the Western assumption that the contract governs everything, was apparently unaware that Mr. Zhang's business culture operates on the opposite assumption: nothing really matters unless it is part of the relationship. Zhang evidently viewed his rock-solid assurance of quality from a *guānxì* partner as superseding anything written in a contract. If Mattel's purchasing agents had cultivated a relationship with Mr. Zhang, they could have asked him to humor their company's obsession with contractual niceties, while reciprocally taking care of Mr. Zhang's needs. The second supply chain link, the *guānxì* partnership between Messrs. Zhang and Liang, was consonant with the culture and did not fail. The most serious breakdown occurred in the culturally inappropriate link between Mr. Liang and the pigment supplier. Because there was no relationship whatever, the usual safeguards against unscrupulous behavior were absent, and Mr. Liang was hoodwinked. This whole, sad affair is traceable to cultural errors along the supply chain.

Garment industry in South Asia

Rana Plaza was a multistory factory complex on the outskirts of Dhaka, Bangladesh. One afternoon in April 2013, garment workers in the building heard a loud noise. A large crack had formed in the building, and an engineer was summoned to inspect it. He took one look and ran out of the building, screaming for everyone to evacuate. However, the landlord Sohel Rana refused to close the building. The factory owners warned workers that they must show up for work the next morning or lose several weeks back pay. It was common practice to delay wages, so that employers could exercise this kind of control over the work force. Shortly after the equipment was switched on the next morning, the building collapsed. No fewer than 1129 workers were killed, and more than 2000 suffered injuries, many of them debilitating for life. It was the worst disaster in the history of the garment industry (DePillis, 2015).

This was not an isolated event. Factory fires in Karachi and Lahore, Pakistan, had killed 289 and 25 workers, respectively, in September 2012 (Guerin, 2012; Karimjee, 2012). Three months later, another fire in Dhaka killed 117 (Ahmed, 2012). The common theme in these disasters was unsafe working conditions, including locked exits to prevent pilferage, a lack of fire extinguishers, and building code violations. Rana's building was likewise non-compliant with local codes. Journalists found evidence in the rubble that high-end and low-end Western retailers were sourcing from these factories, including The Gap, Calvin Klein, KiK Textil-Diskont, and Walmart. Most claimed they knew nothing about the poor working conditions.

A study of one particular supply chain illustrates the nature of the problem. In 2012, Walmart was sourcing garments from Success Apparel, a New York City import-export firm. Success Apparel purchased the garments from Simco in Bangladesh. Simco, in turn, obtained the goods from Tuba Group, another Bangladeshi garment firm. Tuba lacked the capacity to fill Walmart's orders and outsourced them to Tazreen Garment Factory, which was not Walmart-compliant. The unsafe Tazreen factory was the one that burned in Dhaka, killing 117. It was unclear how Walmart or anyone else could have controlled what was happening down this long supply chain.

One strategy often used by Western firms is to rely on third-party inspection and certification, but this, too, is unreliable. The Karachi plant burned, with 289 fatalities, only a month after it had received a prestigious certification from Social Accountability International (SAI), a non-governmental organization that provides ISO certification. This outcome shocked and surprised SAI, but it turned out that the agency had a supply chain problem of its own (Walsh and Greenhouse, 2012). SAI had contracted with an Italian company, RINA Group, to carry out inspections in Pakistan. Yet RINA Group specializes in maritime certification and subcontracted its Karachi inspection work to the Pakistani firm Renaissance Inspection and Certification Agency Pvt. Ltd (RI&CA). The individuals who carried out the inspection for RI&CA evidently "overlooked" serious violations.

The Walmart supply chain crossed the cultural divide between Success Apparel and Simco. From this point on, it was crucial for buyers to cultivate a relationship with suppliers, rather than simply write safety requirements into the contract. Buyers can make sure that suppliers understand the necessity of safe working conditions, and that any lapse could endanger a relationship that may lead to more business in the future. Business people in South Asia are accustomed to relying on relationships to obtain customers, and they will not take safety shortcuts if they understand this would risk losing a profitable relationship. This applies particularly to factory owners, who are pressured by intense cost competition in a low-wage economy. Safety precautions cost money that could drive up costs and risk losing orders. For the sake of the business and its employees, managers must keep costs to a minimum, unless running an unsafe factory would sacrifice relationships that bring them orders. The lesson for Western buyers is obvious enough: in addition to cultivating relationships, be prepared to pay a somewhat higher price to ensure safety.

Maintaining personal contact with suppliers offers another advantage as well. Frequent association naturally leads to information sharing, particularly in a high-context society where information is normally transmitted through the grapevine. Sohel Rana was well known in Dhaka as a corrupt political boss and drug dealer, the sort of figure who might well circumvent building codes by corrupt means. A Western company with person-to-person access to local chatter would avoid suppliers in his building like the plague.

9 Sustainability

What is sustainability?

The most quoted definition of sustainability appears in the Brundtland Report, issued by the World Commission on Environment and Development (1987). It defines sustainable development as "development that meets the needs of the present without compromising the ability of future generations to meet their own needs." This can be viewed as a generalization principle with a focus on the future. It should be possible to achieve the purposes of a given action plan if the plan is universally adopted in the future as well as the present. In fact, as noted in Chapter 7, the generalization principle is already inherently trans-temporal. When testing generalizability, one should suppose an action plan is adopted throughout time, including past, present, and future. There is consequently a sound ethical basis for a sustainability obligation.

Sustainability is frequently conceived as *environmental sustainability*, which is concerned with preserving the natural environment. Yet it also includes *social* and *financial sustainability*, which seek viable social and financial institutions over the long term. Sustainability ideas have long been incorporated in the concept of the *triple bottom line* (Spreckley, 2008), which is a "full cost" approach to accounting that encompasses people, planet, and profit. "People" and "planet" relate to social and environmental sustainability, respectively, and "profit" refers to the traditional bottom line in business. The Global Reporting Initiative (2020), used by thousands of organizations in over 100 countries, has developed standards for measuring the first two bottom lines.

A recent device for assessing sustainability is the *sustainability doughnut* (Raworth, 2017), which represents various social goods as distributed around the circumference of a doughnut, including housing, networks, energy, water, food, health, education, income and work, peace and justice, political voice, social equity, and gender equality. Bars extend into the doughnut hole from each social good to indicate the extent to which we are failing to provide these goods. Other bars extend from each good into the space surrounding the doughnut to show how much we are harming the environment to provide them. In an ideal world, bars would extend in neither direction. Today's doughnut presents a much bleaker picture.

Sustainability is seldom discussed in the business arena without a reference to *greenwashing*. Greenwashing occurs when public relations experts manufacture an apparent concern for the environment, with the aim of attracting environmentally conscious customers. It is often cheaper and easier to appear green than to be green. Greenwashing can be quite subtle, and plastics recycling provides a good example. The proliferation of plastics in the environment has been a concern at least since the first Earth Day in 1970, but the situation continues to worsen. Worldwide use of plastics has increased 20-fold since that time, resulting in the Great Pacific Garbage Patch (Lebreton et al., 2018). There are projections that the world's oceans will contain more plastic than fish by 2050 (World Economic Forum, 2016). Microscopic plastic particles permeate the environment and show up in our food and water, as well as in our bodies (Matei, 2019). One might ask how this can occur, given that so many of us put plastic waste in the recycle bin. The answer is that plastics recycling is and always has been uneconomical, and as a result, only 9 percent of plastics have actually been recycled (Geyer et al., 2017). Much of the plastic we think we are recycling goes to Asia, where it ends up in landfill or the Pacific Ocean. Nonetheless, the plastics industry has long promoted plastics recycling, largely through an advertisement campaign sponsored by the American Chemistry Council. This "greenwashes" the industry by transferring responsibility to the consumer, while the industry itself has been the source of the problem.

Environmental sustainability

Some examples from around the world illustrate how companies and organizations have pursued environmental, social, and financial sustainability. Some of these organizations have received international awards in recognition of their efforts. We begin with environmental sustainability.

A restructured mining company

Umicore began in 1906 as a mining company in Haut Katanga, later known as Belgian Congo, one of the most brutally exploited regions in colonial history. Its practices were the polar opposite of sustainability. Yet today it is a €3.4 billion enterprise known for recycling and environmental responsibility, having been recognized by Corporate Knights as the world's most sustainable company in 2013. The story of this remarkable transformation teaches an important lesson: that the benefits of achieving sustainability are often not what they appear to be (van der Kaaij and Leleux, 2016).

Under the name of Union Minière du Haut Katanga, Umicore got its start by mining copper, tin, and cobalt. By late in the century, the company's growth had stalled. Its reputation was abysmal due to its dark past, and its directors yearned to turn the corner to a brighter future. It changed its name to Umicore in 2001, invested heavily to clean up old mining sites, and began to move away from mining into the *circular economy* (recycling) with an emphasis on automotive catalysts and batteries. It restyled its annual reports, beginning in 2007, to reassure shareholders of the company's long-term focus on sustainability. It noted the growing demand for rechargeable batteries due to the popularity of electric and hybrid cars, and it vowed to contribute to battery recycling. In 2011 it opened a recycling plant in Hoboken, Belgium, and immediately acquired Toyota as a major customer.

By 2019 Umicore was operating in 34 countries with 11,000 employees. Despite this success, its directors were concerned to monetize its new reputation for sustainability. Perhaps positive media exposure could expand market share and convince customers to pay a premium price. Yet the company had already reaped benefits that far exceeded what could be obtained through public relations. An emphasis on sustainability had rescued a declining business, aligned it with today's growing circular economy, and positioned it for further growth in the future. In the process, the company aligned itself with ethics. It met its generalizability obligation while maximizing its utilitarian contribution to the economy of the future.

Coal-fired sustainability?

AES Corporation was founded by Roger Sant and Dennis Bakke in 1981 with the aim of building sustainable coal-fired power plants.[1] This may seem almost a contradiction in terms, and yet, as of 2020, Ethisphere Institute had listed the company among the 130-odd World's Most Ethical Companies for seven years in a row. The company founders recognized that coal was going to remain an important part of the energy landscape for the foreseeable future, and they resolved to make the best of it. Their struggle for simultaneous sustainability and profitability provides an interesting story, particularly its early efforts to offset carbon emissions by planting trees (Trent et al., 1992). It also provides an opportunity to examine more closely the ethics of sustainability.

In 1987, AES was planning its Thames cogeneration plant in Connecticut. It would employ state-of-the-art technology for the time, including fluidized bed combustion, SO_2 sequestration, nitrogen oxide reduction, and the like. However, carbon dioxide (CO_2) remained a problem. Sant, who had become chairman and CEO of the company, asked his staff to examine several options. He specified that the cost should not exceed 1 percent of the plant's total capital cost, and disposal of CO_2 should be permanent. The staff considered CO_2 scrubbers, which were within cost bounds but reduce plant efficiency, and it is difficult to sequester CO_2 permanently. As for alternative fuels, natural gas and wind power were too expensive at the time, hydropower was already exploited, and garbage incineration could release pollutants. The staff eventually recommended planting trees in Guatemala, to reforest 325 square miles of slash-and-burn land. They reasoned that the trees would absorb CO_2 equal to that emitted by the power plant. However, the tree-planting scheme encountered local resistance, and the plant eventually generated

---

[1]   Sant was director of the Energy Productivity Center at my university, Carnegie Mellon, during the period 1977–81. He has exhibited a lifelong interest in energy conservation and environmental issues.

far more carbon than absorbed by reforestation (Wittman and Caron, 2009). This kind of carbon offset was unsustainable in any event, because there was not nearly enough worldwide reforestation potential to absorb future growth in CO_2 emissions. Once a forest reaches full growth, there is little net CO_2 absorption. The carbon becomes part of the biomass, which re-emits CO_2 as dead trees decay.

In essence, this case study asks when it is ethical to improve legacy technology rather than move to new, greener methods. AES could argue that its operations are utilitarian, because it enters markets where only coal-fired energy is cost competitive and displaces less efficient producers. Generalizability (sustainability) is harder to assess. AES could say that it follows a global meta-policy in which some operators improve existing technology, while others explore new technology. The policy is structured to keep worldwide carbon emissions below a growth rate ceiling that is a function of the current atmospheric CO_2 level. The ceiling becomes lower as carbon levels increase over time, but improving technology makes it possible to meet the goal. Such a policy is sustainable if the growth rate ceiling is low enough, and AES could argue that it adheres to what the policy dictates under current conditions. A meta-policy of this sort requires extensive study beyond what is possible here, but it indicates a possible strategy for evaluating the sustainability of companies that rely on fossil fuels.

In the meantime, AES has become one of the world's leading power companies, operating in 15 countries with 8000 employees. Pursuing its interest in sustainability, it partnered with Siemens in 2018 to develop energy storage technologies that could enhance the practicality of wind and solar power. Its recognition as an ethical company may also be related to its organizational culture. Early on, the company resolved to have no mid-level managers or shift supervisors, and to allow worker teams on the plant floor to make most day-to-day decisions. In 2020, it was recognized by the Fast Company as one of the 100 best workplaces for innovators at all levels.

Lease *versus* buy

Our next example is a proposed sustainable business model rather than one that is fully implemented. The proposal is to consider *leasing* household appliances to consumers rather than *selling* the appliances and then trying to recycle material from them (Ellen MacArthur Foundation, 2013). An analysis by McKinsey and Company, for example, showed that leased washing machines can deliver advantages to both manufacturers and consumers while enhancing sustainability. Household machines typically have a life span of less than 10 years while running about 2000 wash cycles, while a high-end leased machine is good for about 10,000 cycles. Consumers who lease a machine can reduce their costs from about $0.27 to $0.12 per cycle, while avoiding the up-front cost of buying the machine. The present value of future costs is reduced by 26–38 percent, depending on the time frame. Meanwhile, the manufacturer obtains a 35 percent improvement in net present value, assuming the machine is leased four times over its 20-year life span. This takes into account a $170 cost of collecting, transporting, and refurbishing the machine after each lease. The manufacturer also enjoys continuous revenue flow that is not subject to the high sensitivity of appliance sales to the business cycle. The sustainability advantages include savings of 180 kg steel and 2.5 tonnes CO_2 per machine, the latter due to the greater efficiency of high-end machines. While an older leased machine will not contain the latest advances in efficiency, many of these advances can be recouped by installing new electronics in the machines during refurbishment. Leasing could therefore be an economically attractive as well as ethical alternative to sales of big-ticket appliances.

Car sharing

Car sharing is the first new business model to emerge in the automotive industry since its inception. It is different from *ride sharing*, in which car owners gives rides to customers. Rather, the customer drives a rented car. Unlike traditional car rental, the customer requests a car using a smart phone app, much as one summons a ride in ride sharing. The customer then picks up the car nearby, perhaps at one of several predefined pick-up points, or wherever the previous driver left the car. The customer need only swipe a card, and the car opens with keys inside. Rental periods can range from an hour to perhaps a week or two. This is a new business model in the sense that manufacturers replace a large portion of customer sales with rentals, resulting in a major change in industry incentives. It could also lead to a more sustainable transportation system if widely adopted.

118 ADVANCED INTRODUCTION TO BUSINESS ETHICS

Car sharing can be peer-to-peer or business-to-customer. Peer-to-peer car sharing, a relatively small segment of the market, allows an individual car owner to share the car. Companies that broker car sharing include Turo, Getaround, and SnappCar. In business-to-customer car sharing, customers drive company-owned cars. The company can be a traditional car rental firm, such as Hertz or Enterprise; a company dedicated to car sharing, such as Zipcar or GoGet; or a manufacturer, such as Ford, Daimler, or BMW (the last two of which operate the joint venture Share Now). The industry is in flux, and it is not clear how it will shake out. General Motors, for example, recently pulled out of the car-sharing business. Car sharing began with such high-end manufacturers as Daimler and BMW, which saw it as an opportunity to expand their business without cutting into their traditional sales to customers, who prefer luxury cars rather than more economical shared cars. Ford, however, is blazing a path into the new business model. On entering the car-sharing market, CEO Mark Fields said, "We are really emphasizing our transition from an auto company to an auto and mobility company...Across the world when you see growth of these megacities, with 10 million or more folks, people want mobility solutions, they want options" (Wilson, 2016). Behind these comments is doubtless a realization that the world's streets and car parks are already jammed with vehicles, a fact that limits future sales growth. Car ownership in a crowded urban environment is increasingly difficult and expensive.

Car sharing offers several potential sustainability advantages.

- Shared cars consume less fuel and produce fewer emissions per mile. The company is incentivized to invest heavily in fuel efficiency because it often pays for the fuel. A customer-owned car, by contrast, incurs primarily fixed costs, because the car is on the road only a couple of hours a day, and there is limited incentive to buy an efficient car.
- Less steel and other materials are required for car manufacture. This is because fewer cars are needed to provide a given number of passenger miles, as the cars are on the road most of the day.
- Less space is tied up in parking, because shared cars are parked a smaller fraction of the time. This reduces the resources necessary to build parking facilities.
- Less parking means that less space on the road is consumed by parked cars, which allows more lanes to open and reduces congestion. Less congestion, in turn, leads to less wasted fuel.

- Customers are incentivized to drive fewer miles, by trip chaining and other means, because transport cost is a variable cost rather than a sunk cost in the vehicle.

A possible disadvantage is that the convenience of car sharing may lure people away from public transportation, which is more efficient than automotive transport. Car sharing also makes a limited contribution during rush hour, which requires a larger fleet of vehicles. One solution is to stagger work hours or allow some employees to work at home near rush hour.

Social sustainability

There is no clear consensus on what is meant by social sustainability. By one definition, a sustainable society should "(1) satisfy an extended set of human needs and (2) [be] shaped in a way that nature and its reproductive capabilities are preserved over a long period of time and the normative claims of social justice, human dignity and participation are fulfilled" (Littig and Griessler, 2005: 72). The precise benefits that a sustainable society should deliver vary from one account to another, but the root idea is that society should be structured to provide these benefits over the long term, without instability or disintegration. The business sector can contribute to social sustainability by adopting policies that are consistent with this goal. The following two case studies recount successful efforts in this direction.

Tea growers in Kenya

The Kenya Tea Development Agency (KTDA) pursues sustainability by promoting social inclusion through worker ownership in the tea industry (Kumar and Satish, 2016). Tea farming and processing is a major sector of the Kenyan economy, involving some 600,000 tea farmers. Jomo Kenyatta established KTDA in 1964 as a government authority after Kenyan independence, and it was privatized as KTDA Ltd. in 2000. One of the agency's early steps was to set up Kenya's own tea auction, to avoid the necessity of middlemen who sold tea on the London auction. Its main innovation was to allow farmers to buy shares in 66 processing plants, paid for by a fraction of their tea production. Farmers elect members of the management boards and earn dividends in addition to revenue from their tea. They receive about 75 percent of the auction price, putting them among the highest-paid small tea farmers in the world. KTDA also sponsors some 4300 field schools that demonstrate efficient farming techniques and sustainable practices. The organization clearly contributes to social sustainability as well as economic prosperity in Kenya.

Affordable housing in Mexico

Vinte is a housing business in Mexico that benefits low-income communities. The name is short for *Viviendas Integrales*, or Integrated Homes. The homes are integrated in the sense that they provide housing along with a number of other amenities, creating a lifestyle that one might associate with a more affluent community (Prasad and Muralidhara, 2014). The aim is to promote greater social inclusion and, with it, sustainability. The company racked up a number of awards in its early years, including the *Financial Times* 2012 Sustainable Investment of the Year, the International Finance Corporation's 2013 Inclusive Business Achievement Award, and multiple National Housing Awards.

A number of features are integrated into Vinte's housing projects. Clean water, paved roads, bicycle paths, and playgrounds are standard. Each project is a walled and gated community with security cameras, located near schools and shopping. Every house comes with a computer and Internet with online grocery ordering. There is Internet access to security cameras from home and work. Most of all, the homes are relatively affordable. Buyers must agree that 5 percent of their paychecks will be deducted, an amount that is applied to the down payment and monthly mortgage payments. Residents tend to be school teachers, secretaries, and factory workers who may have previously lived in unsafe settlements without proper access to water, electricity, and paved roads. A Vinte home is therefore a significant step up. This is a business model that clearly contributes to social and political stability, and therefore sustainability.

Vinte got under way with financial assistance, loans, and bond issues sponsored by the International Finance Corporation, the Inter-American Development Bank, and the German Bank DEG. As of 2019 it had experienced several years of financial success, having built 49,000 homes, and having achieved 36 percent revenue growth over 2017–18.

Financial sustainability

The concept of financial sustainability dates at least back to the 1960s but received particular emphasis in the wake of a series of financial crises: the Asian financial crisis of 1997, the Long-Term Capital Management crisis of 1998, and the global financial crisis of 2008. Critics directed their attention to increasingly complex financial instruments that can mitigate risk for individual investors but may also lead to speculation that destabilizes the financial system. The result was a renewed emphasis on the core purpose of finance: to accumulate capital and put it to work to improve our lives. This gave rise to several principles for sustainable finance:

- The finance industry should promote human welfare, for example by using the triple bottom line as a measure of success.
- Finance should serve the real economy, rather than an artificial world built on securities and derivatives, in part through a focus on local communities.
- The financial system should be stable and emphasize the long term, rather than surrender to short-term speculation.
- Financial institutions should be governed in a transparent and inclusive fashion.

Several organizations have elaborated on these guidelines, including the Global Alliance for Banking on Values (consisting of 66 institutions worldwide), the Sustainable Banking Network (with members in 41 countries), and the U.S. National Community Investment Fund. In addition, some principles of Islamic finance are remarkably parallel to thinking in Western sustainable banking (Spangler, 2013; Myers and Hassanzadeh, 2013). The following statements from CEOs of two leading sustainable banks further clarify the ideas behind sustainable banking.

Triodos Bank is the pioneer in sustainable banking (Dossa et al., 2015; Henderson et al., 2013). Conceived in the 1960s, it finally obtained its Netherlands charter in 1980. The bank's original focus was on socially responsible investing, but it has also been concerned with financial stability and triple-bottom-line assessment. The bank was remarkably unaffected by the 2008 financial crisis. We let CEO Peter Blom speak for

himself, because his reflections comprise as good a manifesto as any for
sustainable banking.

> If banks become the market, they crowd out the real economy because it
> becomes easier to make money with money than by producing things or deliv-
> ering services. Opportunistic investors like banks because they can privatize
> the profits and socialize the losses. That game has been over since 2008, and
> should be over.

> Therefore, there has to be a new idea of what a bank is about...Playing in the
> market, thinking you can make money with money and be very bright in using
> tricks, that's not where you should gain your fulfillment. I think we have to see
> that there can be fulfillment from things like making an entrepreneur success-
> ful, in a serving way...What we have to prove is...that the real economy is as
> exciting as banking that plays with money in abstract markets. (Henderson et
> al., 2013, p. 3)

Vancity is Vancouver City Savings Credit Union. Starting in 1946 with
a $22 investment from founders, it was the first community-wide credit
union in Canada, and today the country's largest. Its emphasis has been
on serving the local community rather than participation in global
financial markets. The organization has received a number of awards,
which in only the last two years include recognition as one of the Best
Corporate Citizens in Canada by Corporate Knights, one of Canada's Top
100 Employers (for the 12th time), one of Canada's Greenest Employers
(for the 10th time), winner of the Highest Customer Service Award in the
banking industry, and recipient of the National Credit Union Innovation
Award. CEO Tamara Vrooman, who stepped down from her position in
mid-2020, summarizes the bank's approach as follows. She will have the
last word in the book.

> The public is calling for changes in the financial system in response to the
> excesses and failures of recent years and increasingly urgent social and envi-
> ronmental challenges. People are hungry to hear about ideas that move us
> beyond the banking meltdown and economic crisis to a banking system that
> values positive impact, integrity, accountability and transparency.

> The opportunity for change is to create a more responsive way to bank, one
> that puts the needs of people and their communities first, and then places
> the tools of banking in service of their economic, social and environmental
> development.

> A study by the Global Alliance for Banking on Values, an independent
> network of the world's leading sustainable banks, proves the point...Across
> almost all the measures that matter in banking, the sustainable banks outper-

formed their peers, with a greater proportion of exposure to customers in both deposits and loans, relatively high and better quality capital, better returns on assets and equal returns on equity with lower volatility of returns, and significantly higher levels of growth…The study concluded overall that sustainable banks were resilient, supported the real economy, and provided stable returns. (Vrooman, 2012)

Appendix

Social welfare functions

A *social welfare function* $W(u_1,...,u_n)$ measures the social value of a given distribution $(u_1,...,u_n)$ of expected utilities over individuals $1,...,n$. The aim is to maximize social welfare subjects to resource constraints. If x_i is the amount of resources allocated to person i, we let $u_i(x_i)$ denote the expected utility of person i when allocated resource amount x_i, where

$$u_i(x_i) = \sum_j p_j u_{ij}(x_i)$$

and where j ranges over possible outcomes, and p_j is the probability of outcome j. We wish to maximize social welfare by solving the problem

$$\max_{x_1,...,x_n} \left\{ W\left(u_1(x_1),...,u_n(x_n)\right) : \sum_{i=1}^{n} x_i \leq R \right\}$$

where R is the resource limit. From here out, we simplify notation by writing $u_i(x_i)$ simply as u_i.

The *utilitarian* social welfare function (SWF) is simply the total net utility

$$W(u_1,...,u_n) = \sum_{i=1}^{n} u_i \ .$$

The *maximin* SWF is

$$W(u_1,\ldots,u_n) = \max\left\{u_i \mid i = 1,\ldots,n\right\}.$$

It is based on the *difference principle* of John Rawls (1971), which states that inequality is acceptable only to the extent that it improves the lot of the worst off. Rawls intended the difference principle to apply to the design of social institutions rather than a general rule for utility distribution. He also intended it only for the distribution of "primary goods," which are goods that every rational person would want. He defended the difference principle with a social contract argument. The argument can be extended to support a *leximax* criterion, which is sensitive to the utility of all disadvantaged persons, not only the very worst off ("leximax" is short for "lexicographic maximum"). The leximax problem first maximizes the utility of the worst-off person, then while holding that utility fixed, maximizes the utility of the second worst-off person, and so forth.

Several SWFs combine utility with equity. Perhaps the best known is *proportional fairness*, which is based on the Nash bargaining solution (Nash, 1950),

$$W(u_1,\ldots,u_n) = \prod_{i=1}^{n} u_i$$

where $u_i > 0$. Nash defends his bargaining solution by showing that it follows from fairly standard axioms of rational choice theory. In addition, Harsanyi (1977), Rubinstein (1982), and Binmore et al. (1986) showed that the Nash solution is the (asymptotic) outcome of certain rational bargaining procedures. However, the axiomatic derivation relies on a strong axiom of cardinal non-comparability across individuals that rules out the kind of utility comparisons needed to assess whether the distribution is satisfactory (Hooker, 2013).

Alpha fairness generalizes proportional fairness with the social welfare function

$$W_\alpha(u_1,\ldots,u_n) = \begin{cases} (1-\alpha)^{-1} \sum_{i=1}^{n} u_i^{1-\alpha}, & \text{if } \alpha \geq 0,\ \alpha \neq 1 \\ \sum_{i=1}^{n} \log u_i, & \text{if } \alpha = 1 \end{cases}.$$

The function is parameterized by a non-negative number α and is equivalent to proportional fairness when $\alpha = 1$. It becomes a purely utilitarian criterion when $\alpha = 0$ and a Rawlsian maximin criterion for sufficiently large α, with larger values of α implying a greater emphasis on equity. The parameter α can be interpreted as quantifying the equity/efficiency trade-off, because the utility u_j of person j must be reduced by $(u_j/u_i)^\alpha$ units to compensate for a unit increase in u_i $(< u_j)$ while maintaining constant social welfare.

Since the maximin criterion captures an important notion of fairness, it may be desirable to combine it with a utilitarian criterion to obtain an alternate approach to balancing equity and efficiency. One scheme for combining them is that of Hooker and Williams (2012), which uses a parameter Δ to regulate the equity/efficiency trade-off. The SWF can be written

$$W_\Delta(u_1,\ldots,u_n) = (n-1)\Delta + nu_{\min} + \sum_{i=1}^{n} \max\left\{0,\ u_i - u_{\min} - \Delta\right\}$$

where $u_{\min} = \min_i u_i$. This criterion is purely utilitarian when $\Delta = 0$ and purely Rawlsian for sufficiently large Δ. The trade-off parameter Δ may be easier to interpret in practice than α, because the SWF gives greater weight to individuals whose utility is within Δ of the lowest. Decision makers can therefore determine how near the worst off a person must be before receiving special consideration. Hooker and Williams show that maximizing the SWF can be formulated as a mixed integer/linear programming (MILP) problem that is easily solved in practice. Utilitarianism can also be combined with a leximax criterion rather than a maximin criterion to account for equity more adequately (Chen and Hooker, 2020). The resulting SWF can be maximized by solving a sequence of MILP problems.

Still another approach to balancing equity and efficiency is the Kalai–Smorodinsky bargaining solution, which, like the Nash solution, has an axiomatic derivation (Kalai and Smorodinsky, 1975). It begins by noting the current or default allocation $(d_1,\ldots,d_n)$ of utilities and the maximum utility $u_i^{\max}$ each person could have if everyone else had only the default amount. The goal is to maximize total utility under the constraint that each person experiences the same relative concession. That is, each person receives the same fraction β of the gap between the default and maximum utilities. So the SWF is the utilitarian function, and the maximization problem can be written

$$\max_{\beta, x_1, \ldots, x_n} \left\{ \sum_{i=1}^{n} u_i(x_i) : \sum_{i=1}^{n} x_i \leq R; \; u_i(x_i) = (1-\beta)d_i + \beta u_i^{\max}, \text{ all } i; \; 0 \leq \beta \leq 1 \right\}$$

where

$$u_i^{\max} = \max_{x_1, \ldots, x_n} \left\{ u_i(x_i) : \sum_{j=1}^{n} x_j \leq R; \; u_j(x_j) \geq d_j, \text{ all } j \right\}.$$

In the bargaining derivation of this formulation, the default utility d_i is the position on which the parties fall back if bargaining fails. The resulting distribution reflects the contractarian ethical philosophy of Gautier (1983). Despite the bargaining argument, the Kalai–Smorodinsky has a counterintuitive implication (Hooker, 2013). If one person's utility gain is very expensive and so requires large utility transfers from others, the others are forced to accept very small utility gains when much greater overall utility gains are possible.

Statistical fairness metrics

To formulate statistical (group) fairness measures, we adopt the following fairly standard notation. Let $Y \in \{0,1\}$ be the correct classification of a given individual, and let . $\hat{Y} \in \{0,1\}$. be the classification predicted by an AI system. We say that the individual is *qualified* when $Y = 1$ and *selected* when $\hat{Y} = 1$. Let $Z = 1$ when the individual belongs to a protected class, and $Z = 0$ otherwise. Finally, let $P(\hat{Y} = \hat{y} \mid Y = y)$ be the conditional probability that $\hat{Y} = \hat{y}$ given that $Y = y$. The major statistical fairness measures are as follows:

- *Demographic parity.* $P(\hat{Y} = \hat{y} \mid Z = 1) = P(\hat{Y} = \hat{y} \mid Z = 0)$ for $\hat{y} = 0, 1$ and $y = 0, 1$. This rules out a perfect predictor $\hat{Y} = Y$ when the fraction of qualified individuals in the protected group is different from the fraction of qualified individuals in the unprotected group; that is, when $P(Y = 1 \mid Z = 1) \neq P(Y = 1 \mid Z = 0)$.

- *Equalized odds.* $P(\hat{Y} = \hat{y} \mid Y = y, Z = 1) = P(\hat{Y} = \hat{y} \mid Y = y, Z = 0)$ for $\hat{y} = 0,1$ and $y = 0,1$. A weaker form of this condition is *equality of opportunity*: $P(\hat{Y} = 1 \mid Y = 1, Z = 1) = P(\hat{Y} = 1 \mid Y = 1, Z = 0)$.

- *Predictive rate parity.* $P(Y = y \mid \hat{Y} = \hat{y}, Z = 1) = P(Y = y \mid \hat{Y} = \hat{y}, Z = 0)$, for $y = 0,1$ and $\hat{y} = 0,1$.

- *Counterfactual fairness.* To define this condition, we let X be the vector of features used to classify an individual. We must also identify a vector U of characteristics that are not directly observable but that have a causal influence on Y while having no causal influence on the protected status Z. Then the selection of a given individual must depend solely on U. Using the (somewhat confusing) notation of Kusner et al. (2017), the counterfactual fairness condition

$$P\left(\hat{Y}(U)_{Z \leftarrow z} = \hat{y} \mid X = x, Z = z\right) = P\left(\hat{Y}(U)_{Z \leftarrow z'} = \hat{y} \mid X = x, Z = z\right)$$

for $\hat{y} = 0,1$, $z = 0,1$, $z' = 0,1$, and for all vectors x. This is intended to say that the probability of selecting or rejecting a given individual with a given set of features would be the same in an alternate possible world in which that individual has underlying characteristics U but has protected status z' rather than z. Kusner et al. use Bayesian inference in causal networks to infer the causal influence of the hidden factors U (Pearl, 2000; Pearl et al., 2016).

References

Ahmed, F. (2012). At least 117 killed in fire at Bangladeshi clothing factory. *CNN*, November 25.

Allen, A. (2011). *Unpopular Privacy: What Must We Hide?* Oxford: Oxford University Press.

Alphabet, Inc. (2020). *Google Code of Conduct.* https://abc.xyz/investor/other/google-code-of-conduct, accessed November 22, 2020.

Altman, I. (1977). Privacy regulation: Culturally universal or culturally specific? *Journal of Social Issues*, **33**, 66–84.

Anscombe, G. E. M. (1958). Modern moral philosophy. *Philosophy*, **33**, 1–19.

Australian Associated Press. (2012). Leighton wins $515m Dubai hotel contract. *Sydney Morning Herald*, February 21.

Awad, E. (2019). Your (future) car's moral compass. *Behavioral Scientist*, February 11.

Barboza, D. (2007). Scandal and suicide in China: A dark side of toys. *New York Times*, August 23.

BBC. (2020). France: Bus driver dies after "attack over face masks" in Bayonne. *BBC News*, July 10.

Bentham, J. (1780). Of the principle of utility. In *An Introduction to the Principles of Morals and Legislation*. London: T. Payne and Sons, 1–6.

Bentham, J. (1787). *The Panopticon Writings*. London: Verso Books, reprinted 1995.

Bernays, E. L. (1923). *Crystallizing Public Opinion*. New York: Boni and Liveright.

Bilgrami, A. (2006). *Self-Knowledge and Resentment*. Cambridge, MA: Harvard University Press.

Binmore, K., Rubinstein, A., and Wolinsky, A. (1986). The Nash bargaining solution in economic modeling. *RAND Journal of Economics*, **17**, 176–88.

Binns, R. (2018). Fairness in machine learning: Lessons from political philosophy. *Journal of Machine Learning Research*, **81**, 1–11.

Boisjoly, R. P., Curtis, E. F., and Mellican, E. (1989). Roger Boisjoly and the Challenger disaster: The ethical dimensions. *Journal of Business Ethics*, **8**, 217–30. The first author is brother of the late Roger Boisjoly.

Brandom, R. (2018). Self-driving cars are headed toward an AI roadblock. *The Verge*, July 3.

Bresch, H. (2016). *Testimony before U.S. House of Representatives Committee on Oversight and Government Reform*. Washington, DC: U.S. Government Publishing Office, September 21.

Brynjolfsson, E., and McAfee, A. (2014). *The Second Machine Age: Work, Progress and Prosperity in a Time of Brilliant Technologies.* New York: W. W. Norton.

Burdín, G. (2014). Are worker-managed firms more likely to fail than conventional enterprises? Evidence from Uruguay. *Industrial and Labor Relations Review,* **67**, 202–38.

Chamorro-Mera, A. (2018). Analysis of the predictive variables of the intention to invest in a socially responsible manner. *Journal of Cleaner Production,* **196**, 469–77.

Chappell, B., and Wamsley, L. (2018). Amazon sets $15 minimum wage for U.S. employees, including temps. *National Public Radio,* October 2.

Chen, V., and Hooker, J. N. (2020). Balancing fairness and efficiency in an optimization model. *ArXiv* preprint 2006.05963.

Christakis, N. A. (2019). How AI will rewire us. *Atlantic,* April, 10–13.

Clark, L. (2020). Amazon settles for $11m with workers in unpaid bag-search wait lawsuit. *The Register,* May 1.

Clement, J. (2020). Cyber crime: Number of breaches and records exposed 2005–2020. *Statistica,* October 1.

Cohen, J. (2002). *Regulating Intimacy: A New Legal Paradigm.* Princeton, NJ: Princeton University Press.

Davenport, T. H., and Kirby, J. (2015). Beyond automation. *Harvard Business Review,* **93**(6), 59–65.

Davidson, D. (1963). Actions, reasons, and causes. *Journal of Philosophy,* **60**, 685–700.

DePillis, L. (2015). Two years ago, 1129 people died in a Bangladesh factory collapse. The problems still haven't been fixed. *Washington Post,* April 23.

Dossa, Z., Kaeufer, K., and Szekely, F. (2015). *Triodos Bank: Measuring Sustainability Performance.* Lausanne: International Institute for Management Development, Case IMD-7-1738.

Dwork, C., Hardt, M., Pitassi, T., Reingold, O., and Zemel, R. (2012). Fairness through awareness. *Proceedings of 3rd Innovations in Theoretical Computer Science Conference,* 214–26.

Eastman Kodak Company. (2019). *Kodak Business Conduct Guide,* November. www.kodak.com/content/products-brochures/Company/business-conduct -guide-en.pdf, accessed November 22, 2020.

Ellen MacArthur Foundation. (2013). *Towards the Circular Economy: Economic and Business Rationale for an Accelerated Transition.* Cowes.

Engelbart, D. C. (1962). Augmenting human intellect: A conceptual framework. *SRI Summary Report AFOSR-3223.* Prepared for Director of Information Sciences, Air Force Office of Scientific Research, Washington, DC.

Foot, P. (1967). The problem of abortion and the doctrine of double effect. *Oxford Review,* **5**, 5–15; reprinted in B. Steinbock and A. Norcross, eds, *Killing and Letting Die,* 2nd ed. New York: Fordham University Press (1994), 266–79.

Francis, L. P., and Francis, J. G. (2017). *Privacy: What Everyone Needs to Know.* Oxford: Oxford University Press.

Frank, A. (1947). *Het Achterhuis. Dagboekbrieven 14 Juni 1942–1 Augustus 1944.* Translated by B. M. Mooyaart as *The Diary of a Young Girl.* New York: Bantam Books, 1993.

Freeman, R. E. (1983). *Strategic Management: A Stakeholder Approach*. Boston, MA: Pitman.

Friedman, M. (1962). *Capitalism and Freedom*. Chicago, IL: University of Chicago Press.

Friedman, M. (1970). The social responsibility of business is to increase its profits. *New York Times Magazine*, September 13.

Gautier, D. (1983). *Morals by Agreement*. Oxford: Oxford University Press.

Gerstein, R. (1978). Intimacy and privacy. *Ethics*, **89**, 76–81.

Geyer, R., Jambeck, J. R., and Law, K. L. (2017). Production, use, and fate of all plastics ever made. *Science Advances*, 3, July 19.

Gioia, D. (1992). Pinto fires and personal ethics: A script analysis of missed opportunities. *Journal of Business Ethics*, **11**, 379–89.

Global Reporting Initiative. (2020). *GRI Standards*. www.globalreporting.org, accessed January 25, 2020.

Goodman, N. (1955). *Fact, Fiction and Forecast*. Cambridge, MA: Harvard University Press.

Goodpaster, K. E. (1991). Business ethics and stakeholder analysis. *Business Ethics Quarterly*, **1**, 53–73.

Guerin, O. (2012). Death toll from Karachi factory fire soars. *BBC News*, September 12.

Hall, E. T. (1959). *The Silent Language*. New York: Anchor Books.

Hall, E. T. (1966). *The Hidden Dimension*. New York: Anchor Books.

Hall, E. T. (1983). *The Dance of Life: The Other Dimension of Time*. New York: Anchor Books.

Hardt, M., Price, E., and Srebro, N. (2016). Equality of opportunity in supervised learning. *Proceedings of 30th International Conference on Neural Information Processing*, 3323–31.

Harman, G. (1977). *The Nature of Morality*. New York: Oxford University Press.

Harman, G. (1999). Moral philosophy meets social psychology: Virtue ethics and the fundamental attribution error. *Proceedings of the Aristotelian Society* (New Series), **119**, 316–31.

Harman, G. (2003). No character or personality. *Business Ethics Quarterly*, **13**, 87–94.

Harsanyi, J. C. (1977). *Rational Behavior and Bargaining Equilibrium in Games and Social Situations*. Cambridge: Cambridge University Press.

Hayek, F. A. (1960). *The Constitution of Liberty*. Chicago, IL: University of Chicago Press.

Heales, C., Hodgson, M., and Rich, H. (2017). *Humanity at Work: Mondragon, A Social Innovation Ecosystem Case Study*. London: Young Foundation.

Hellsten, S., and Mallin, C. (2006). Are "ethical" or "socially responsible" investments socially responsible? *Journal of Business Ethics*, **66**, 393–406.

Henderson, R., Isaacs, K., and Kaufer, K. (2013). *Triodos Bank: Conscious Money in Action*. Cambridge, MA: Harvard Business School, Case study 313-109.

Hofstede, G. (1980). *Culture's Consequences: International Differences in Work-Related Values*. Thousand Oaks, CA: Sage Publishing.

Hofstede, G., Hofstede, G. J., and Minkov, M. (2010). *Cultures and Organizations: Software of the Mind*, 3rd ed. New York: McGraw-Hill.

Hooker, J. N. (2003). *Working across Cultures*. Redwood City, CA: Stanford University Press.

Hooker, J. N. (2009). Corruption from a cross-cultural perspective. *Cross-Cultural Management: An International Journal*, **16**, 251–67.

Hooker, J. N. (2012). Cultural differences in business communication. In C. B. Paulston, S. F. Kiesling, and E. S. Rangel, eds, *Handbook of Intercultural Discourse and Communication*. New York: Wiley, 389–407.

Hooker, J. N. (2013). Moral implications of rational choice theories. In C. Lütge, ed., *Handbook of the Philosophical Foundations of Business Ethics*. Berlin: Springer, 1459–76.

Hooker, J. N. (2014). Bridging a supply chain's cultural divide. *Inside Supply Management*, first quarter, 34–6.

Hooker, J. N. (2018). *Taking Ethics Seriously: Why Ethics Is an Essential Tool for the Modern Workplace*. Abingdon-on-Thames: Taylor and Francis.

Hooker, J. N., and Kim, T. W. (2019). Ethical implications of the 4th Industrial Revolution for business and society. In D. Wasileski and J. Weber, eds, *Business and Society 360, Vol. 3: Business Ethics*. Bingley: Emerald Group Publishing, 35–63.

Hooker, J. N., and Kim, T. W. (forthcoming). Humanizing business in the age of artificial intelligence. In M. Dion, E. Freeman and S. Dmytriyev, eds, *Humanizing Business: What Humanities Can Say to Business*. Berlin: Springer.

Hooker, J. N., and Williams, H. P. (2012). Combining equity and utilitarianism in a mathematical programming model. *Management Science*, **58**, 1682–93.

House, R. J., Hanges, P. J., Javidan, M., Dorfman, P. W., and Gupta, V., eds. (2004). *Culture, Leadership and Organizations: The GLOBE Study of 62 Societies*. Thousand Oaks, CA: Sage Publishing.

House, R. J., Dorfman, P. W., Javidan, M., Hanges, P. J., and Sully de Luque, M. F. (2014). *Strategic Leadership across Cultures: The GLOBE Study of CEO Leadership Behavior and Effectiveness in 24 Countries*. Thousand Oaks, CA: Sage Publishing.

Hume, D. (1739). *A Treatise of Human Nature*. Reprinted as *A Treatise of Human Nature: A Critical Edition*, D. F. Norton and M. J. Norton, eds. Oxford: Clarendon Press (2007).

IBM. (2020). *AI Fairness 360*. https://aif360.mybluemix.net, accessed December 16, 2020.

Inness, J. (1992). *Privacy, Intimacy and Isolation*. Oxford: Oxford University Press.

International Cooperative Alliance. (2020). Cooperative identity, values and principles. www.ica.coop/en/cooperatives/cooperative-identity, accessed November 16, 2020.

Jensen, M. C., and Meckling, W. H. (1976). Theory of the firm: Managerial behavior, agency costs and ownership structure. *Journal of Financial Economics*, **3**, 305–60.

Kagan, S. (1989). *The Limits of Morality*. Oxford: Clarendon Press.

Kahneman, D. (2011). *Thinking, Fast and Slow*. New York: Farrar, Straus and Giroux.

Kalai, E., and Smorodinsky, M. (1975). Other solutions to Nash's bargaining problem. *Econometrica*, **43**, 513–18.

Kant, I. (1785). *Grundlegung zur Metaphysik der Sitten* (*Foundations of the Metaphysics of Morals*). Reprinted in *Kants gesammelte Schriften*, Vol. 4, Königlichen Preußischen Akademie der Wissenschaften. Berlin: Georg Reimer (1900).

Kant, I. (1797). On a supposed right to lie from philanthropy. Originally published in *Berlinische Blätter*, 1799. Translated by L. W. Beck in *Critique of Practical Reason and Other Writings in Moral Philosophy*. Chicago, IL: University of Chicago Press, 1949, 346–50.

Karimjee, M. (2012). Pakistan: Factory fires kill over 300 people. *Agence France-Presse*, September 12.

Kaswan, M. J. (2019). Happiness theory and worker cooperatives: A critique of the alignment thesis. *Journal of Labor and Society*, **22**, 637–60.

Kenney, B. (2007). How the Mattel fiasco really happened. *Industry Week*, September 6. www.industryweek.com/innovation/article/22010797/how-the-mattel-fiasco-really-happened, accessed January 19 2021.

Kierkegaard, S. (1843). *Frygt og Bæven*. English translation: *Fear and Trembling*. Translated by A. Hannay. London: Penguin Books, 2006.

Kim, H. J., Hooker, J. N., and Donaldson, T. (2021). Taking principles seriously: A hybrid approach to value alignment. *Journal of Artificial Intelligence Research*, **70**, 871–90.

Kim, R., Kleiman-Weiner, M., Abeliuk, A., Awad, E., Dsouza, S., Tenenbaum, J. B., and Rahwan, I. (2018). A computational model of commonsense moral decision making. *Proceedings, AAAI/ACM Conference on AI, Ethics, and Society*, 197–203.

Kluger, B. D., and Slezak, S. L. (2018). Signal jamming models of fraudulent misreporting and economic prospects: An experimental investigation. *Journal of Economic Behavior and Organization*, **151**, 254–83.

Korsgaard, C. M. (1996). *The Sources of Normativity*. Cambridge: Cambridge University Press.

Kumar, N., and Satish, D. (2016). *KTDAL: Building Sustainability through Inclusion*. Hyderabad: IBS Centre for Management Research.

Kupfer, J. (1987). Privacy, autonomy and self-concept. *American Philosophical Quarterly*, **24**, 81–9.

Kusner, M. J., Loftus, J., Russell, C., and Silva, R. (2017). Counterfactual fairness. *Proceedings of Advances in Neural Information Processing Systems*, 4069–79.

Kwon, M., Jung, M. F., and Knepper, R. A. (2016). Human expectations of social robots. *11th ACM/IEEE International Conference on Human–Robot Interaction*, 463–64.

Lebreton, L. et al. (2018). Evidence that the Great Pacific garbage patch is rapidly accumulating plastic. *Scientific Reports*, **8**, 4666.

Lewis, D. (2001). *Counterfactuals*. New York: Wiley-Blackwell.

Lief, C., and Ward, J. L. (2008). *Lee Kum Kee Co. Ltd (A): The Family Recipe*. Case IMD-3-1617. Lausanne: International Institute for Management Development.

Liptak, A. (2014). Supreme Court rules against worker pay for screenings in Amazon warehouse case. *New York Times*, December 9.

Littig, B., and Griessler, E. (2005). Social sustainability: A catchword between political pragmatism and social theory. *International Journal of Sustainable Development*, **8**, 65–79.

MacIntyre, A. (1985). *After Virtue*. London: Duckworth.

Marsh, R., and Wallace, G. (2019). Whistleblower testifies that Boeing ignored pleas to shut down 737 Max production. *CNN*, December 11.

Matei, A. (2019). Those fancy tea bags? Microplastics in them are macro offenders. *The Guardian*, September 30.

McKenzie, N. (2020). How an international bribes scandal, a cover-up and a trove of leaked emails ended in a suburban Brisbane arrest. *Sydney Morning Herald*, November 18.

McKenzie, N., and Baker, R. (2013). Building giant Leighton rife with corruption: Claims. *Sydney Morning Herald*, October 3.

Meyer, B. (2005). Maker of heart device kept flaw from doctors. *New York Times*, May 24.

Meyers, C. (2004). Wrongful beneficence: Exploitation and third-world sweatshops. *Journal of Social Philosophy*, **35**, 319–33.

Mill, J. S. (1863). *Utilitarianism*. In J. M. Robson, ed., *The Collected Works of John Stuart Mill*, Vol. 10. Toronto: University of Toronto Press, 1963–91.

Mishel, L., and Kandra, J. (2020). *CEO Compensation Surged 14% in 2019 to $21.3 Million*. Washington, DC: Economic Policy Institute, August 18.

MIT Media Lab (2020). *Moral Machine*. www.moralmachine.net, accessed December 29, 2020.

Mitchell, M. S., Reynolds, S. J., and Treviño, L. K. (2020). The study of behavioral ethics within organizations: A special issue introduction. *Personnel Psychology*, **73**, 5–17.

Mitroff, I. (1983). *Stakeholders of the Organizational Mind*. San Francisco, CA: Jossey-Bass.

Moore, A. D. (2010). *Privacy Rights: Moral and Legal Foundations*. University Park, PA: Penn State University Press.

Moore, G. E. (1903). *Principia Ethica*. Cambridge: Cambridge University Press.

Mulgan, T. (2001). *The Demands of Consequentialism*. Oxford: Clarendon Press.

Mullins, J., and Rhodes, T. (2011). Managing ethically in corrupt environments. *Business Strategy Review*, **4**, 50–5.

Munde, G. (1995). *Report of the Cabinet Subcommittee to Review the Dabhol Power Project*. Government of Maharashtra State, India.

Murphy, L. (2000). *Moral Demands in Nonideal Theory*. New York: Oxford University Press.

Myers, T. A., and Hassanzadeh, E. (2013). *The Interconnections between Islamic Finance and Sustainable Finance*. Winnipeg: International Institute for Sustainable Development.

Nagel, T. (1986). *The View from Nowhere*. Oxford: Oxford University Press.

Nash, J. (1950). The bargaining problem. *Econometrica*, **18**, 155–62.

Nelkin, D. K. (2000). Two standpoints and the belief in freedom. *Journal of Philosophy*, **97**, 564–76.

Nissenbaum, H. (2010). *Privacy in Context: Technology, Policy, and the Integrity of Social Life*. Redwood City, CA: Stanford University Press.

Norcross, A. (1997). Comparing harms: Headaches and human lives. *Philosophy and Public Affairs*, **26**, 135–67.

O'Neil, C. (2017). *Weapons of Math Destruction*. New York: Broadway Books.

O'Neill, O. (2014). *Acting on Principle: An Essay on Kantian Ethics*, 2nd ed. Cambridge: Cambridge University Press.

Olsen, E. (2013). The relative survival of worker cooperatives and barriers to their creation. *Advances in the Economic Analysis of Participatory and Labor-Managed Firms*, **14**, 83–107.

Organisation for Economic Co-operation and Development. (2020). Temporary employment. https://data.oecd.org/emp/temporary-employment.htm, accessed December 1, 2020.

Packard, V. (1957). *The Hidden Persuaders*. New York: David McKay Co.

Palmer, A. (2020). Amazon says more than 19,000 workers got Covid-19. *CNBC*, October 1.

Palmer, T. (2019). State of the sector: US worker cooperatives in 2017. *Journal of Participation and Employee Ownership*, **2**, 190–201.

Parent, W. (1983). Privacy, morality, and the law. *Philosophy and Public Affairs*, **12**, 269–88.

Pearl, J. (2000). *Causality: Models, Reasoning and Inference*. Cambridge: Cambridge University Press.

Pearl, J., Glymour, M., and Jewell, N. (2016). *Causal Inference in Statistics: A Primer*. New York: Wiley.

Pérotin, V. (2016). What do we really know about workers' co-operatives? In T. Webster, L. Shaw, and R. Vorberg-Rugh, eds, *Mainstreaming Co-operation: An Alternative for the Twenty-first Century?* Manchester: Manchester University Press, 239–60.

Piper, K. (2018). "Impact investment" funds advertise great returns and social impacts. They aren't delivering. *Vox*, December 19.

Pollack, A. (2015). Drug goes from $13.50 a tablet to $750, overnight. *New York Times*, September 20.

Prasad, N. V., and Muralidhara, G. V. (2014). *Mexico's Vinte – Affordable and Sustainable Housing for BOP Customers*. Hyderabad: IBS Centre for Management Research.

Press Trust of India. (2019). Enron-Dabhol power project: Supreme Court closes case of alleged corruption. *Economic Times*, April 11.

Rawls, J. (1951). Outline of a decision procedure for ethics. *Philosophical Review*, **60**, 177–97.

Rawls, J. (1971). *A Theory of Justice*. Cambridge, MA: Harvard University Press. 2nd ed. 1999.

Raworth, K. (2017). *Doughnut Economics: Seven Ways to Think Like a 21st Century Economist*. White River Junction, VT: Chelsea Green Publishing.

Reiman, J. (2004). Driving to the Panopticon: A philosophical exploration of the risks to privacy posed by the information technology of the future. In B. Rössler, ed., *Privacies: Philosophical Evaluations*. Stanford, CA: Stanford University Press, 194–214.

Ricard, M. (2015). *Altruism: The Power of Compassion to Change Yourself and the World*. New York: Little, Brown and Company.

Rivoli, P. (2003). Making a difference or making a statement? Finance research and socially responsible investment. *Business Ethics Quarterly*, **13**, 271–87.

Rosenthal, E. (2017). *An American Sickness: How Healthcare Became Big Business and How You Can Take It Back*. New York: Penguin Press.

Rössler, B. (2015). Should personal data be a tradable good? On the moral limits of markets in privacy. In B. Rössler and D. Mokrosinska, eds, *Social Dimensions of Privacy: Interdisciplinary Perspectives*. Cambridge: Cambridge University Press, 141–61.

Rubinstein, A. (1982). Perfect equilibrium in a bargaining model. *Econometrica*, **50**, 97–109.

Russell, C., Kusner, M. J., Loftus, J. R., and Silva, R. (2017). When worlds collide: Integrating different counterfactual assumptions in fairness. *Proceedings of 31st International Conference on Neural Information Processing Systems*, 6417–26.

Sahlins, M. (1963). Poor man, rich man, big man, chief: Political types in Melanesia and Polynesia. *Comparative Studies in Society and History*, **5**, 285–303.

Sandbu, M. E., and Wen, J. (2008). Dicing with death? A case study of Guidant Corporation's implantable defibrillator business. Wharton School, University of Pennsylvania. Reprinted in W. M. Hoffmann, R. E. Frederick, and M. S., Schwartz, eds, *Business Ethics: Readings and Cases in Corporate Morality*. New York: Wiley (2014), 636–42.

Scanlon, T. (1975). Thomson on privacy. *Philosophy and Public Affairs*, **4**, 295–314.

Schwab, K. (2016). *The Fourth Industrial Revolution*. New York: Crown Publishing Group.

Signori, S. (2020). Socially responsible investors. In L. San-Jose, J. L. Retolaza, and L. van Liedekerke, eds, *Handbook on Ethics and Finance*. Berlin: Springer, 285–304.

Singer, P. (1972). Famine, affluence, and morality. *Philosophy and Public Affairs*, **1**, 229–43.

Smith, A. (1759, last revised 1790). *The Theory of Moral Sentiments*. Reprinted in K. Haakonssen, ed. Cambridge: Cambridge University Press (2002).

Smith, A. (1776, last revised 1789). *An Inquiry into the Nature and Causes of the Wealth of Nations*. Reprinted 1977. Chicago: University of Chicago Press.

Snyder, A., Alsharif, M., and Waldrop, T. (2020). Three family members charged in shooting death of security guard who told a customer to put on a face mask. *CNN*, May 5.

Sobel, D. (2007). The impotence of the demandingness objection. *Philosophers' Imprint*, **7**, 1–17.

Spangler, T. (2013). Could principles of Islamic finance feed into a sustainable economic system? *The Guardian*, October 18.

Spencer, H. (1864). *Principles of Biology*, Vol. 1. London: Williams and Norgate.

Spreckley, F. (2008). *Social Audit Toolkit*, 4th ed. St. Oswald's Barn: Local Livelihoods.

Squires, S. E., Smith, C. J., McDougall, L., and Yeack, W. R. (2003). *Inside Arthur Andersen: Shifting Values, Unexpected Consequences*. London: Financial Times Press.

Summers, J., and Chillas, S. (2019). Working in employee-owned companies: The role of economic democracy skills. *Economic and Industrial Democracy*, March 21.

Sussman. D. (2009). On the supposed duty of truthfulness. In C. W. Martin, ed., *The Philosophy of Deception*. New York: Oxford University Press, 225–43.

Thomson, J. J. (1975). The right to privacy. *Philosophy and Public Affairs*, **4**, 295–314.

Thomson, J. J. (1976). Killing, letting die, and the trolley problem. *The Monist*, **59**, 204–17.

Trent, M., Post, J. E., Reinhardt, F., and Scott, W. D. (1992). *The AES Corporation, (A) and (B)*. Washington, DC: World Resources Institute.

Trianosky, G. V. (1990). What is virtue ethics all about? American Philosophical Quarterly, 27, 335–44. Reprinted in D. Statman, ed., *Virtue Ethics*. Cambridge: Edinburgh University Press (1997), 145–64.

U.S. Bureau of Labor Statistics. (2018). *Contingent and Alternative Employment Arrangements – May 2017*. Washington, DC: U.S. Department of Labor.

Unger, P. K. (1996). *Living High and Letting Die*. New York: Oxford University Press.

van der Kaaij, J., and Leleux, B. (2016). *Umicore's Transformation and the Monetizing of Sustainability*. Lausanne: International Institute for Management Development, Case IMD-7-1708.

Van Dijk-de Groot, M., and Nijhof, A. H. J. (2015). Socially responsible investment funds: A review of research priorities and strategic options. *Journal of Sustainable Finance and Investment*, **5**, 178–204.

Varden, H. (2010). Kant and lying to the murderer at the door…one more time: Kant's legal philosophy and lies to murderers and Nazis. *Journal of Social Philosophy*, **41**, 403–21.

Vieta, M., Quarter, J., Spear, R., and Moskovskaya, A. (2016). Participation in worker cooperatives. In *The Palgrave Handbook of Volunteering, Civic Participation, and Nonprofit Associations*. London: Palgrave Macmillan, 436–53.

Vinik, D. (2018). The real future of work. *Politico Magazine*, January–February.

Viswanatha, A., and LaCapra, L. T. (2013). U.S. government slams S&P with $5 billion fraud lawsuit. *Reuters*, February 5.

Vrooman, T. (2012). Opinion: Banking pursues greener pastures. *Vancouver Sun*, December 27.

Wall, J. F. (1989). *Andrew Carnegie*. Pittsburgh, PA: University of Pittsburgh Press.

Walsh, D., and Greenhouse, S. (2012). Inspectors certified Pakistani factory as safe before disaster. *New York Times*, September 20.

Warren, S., and Brandeis, L. D. (1890). The right to privacy. *Harvard Law Review*, **4**, 193–220.

Williams, B. (1985). *Ethics and the Limits of Philosophy*. London: Fontana.

Wilson, E. O. (1975). *Sociobiology: The New Synthesis*. Cambridge, MA: Harvard University Press.

Wilson, J. (2016). Ford CEO looks to autonomous cars, sharing economy. *Phys. org News*, February 22.

Wittman, H., and Caron, C. (2009). Carbon offsets and inequality: Social costs and co-benefits in Guatemala and Sri Lanka. *Society and Natural Resources*, **22**, 710–26.

World Commission on Environment and Development. (1987). *Our Common Future*. Oxford: Oxford University Press.

World Economic Forum. (2016). *The New Plastics Economy: Rethinking the Future of Plastics*. Cologny.

Zafar, M. B., Valera, I., Rodrigues, M. G., and Gummadi, K. P. (2017). Fairness beyond disparate treatment and disparate impact: Learning classification without disparate mistreatment. *Proceedings of 26th International Conference on World Wide Web*, 1171–80.

Index

Titles in the **Elgar Advanced Introductions** series include:

International Human Rights Law
Second Edition
Dinah L. Shelton

Law and Artificial Intelligence
*Woodrow Barfield and
Ugo Pagello*

Politics of International
Human Rights
David P. Forsythe

Community-based Conservation
Fikret Berkes

Global Production Networks
Neil M. Coe

Mental Health Law
Michael L. Perlin

Law and Literature
Peter Goodrich

Creative Industries
John Hartley

Global Administration Law
Sabino Cassese

Housing Studies
William A.V. Clark

Global Sports Law
Stephen F. Ross

Public Policy
B. Guy Peters

Empirical Legal Research
Herbert M. Kritzer

Cities
Peter J. Taylor

Law and Entrepreneurship
Shubha Ghosh

Mobilities
Mimi Sheller

Technology Policy
*Albert N. Link and James A.
Cunningham*

Urban Transport Planning
Kevin J. Krizek and David A. King

Legal Reasoning
*Larry Alexander and Emily
Sherwin*

Sustainable Competitive
Advantage in Sales
Lawrence B. Chonko

Law and Development
Second Edition
*Mariana Mota Prado and Michael
J. Trebilcock*

Law and Renewable Energy
Joel B. Eisen

Experience Economy
Jon Sundbo

Marxism and Human Geography
Kevin R. Cox

Maritime Law
Paul Todd

American Foreign Policy
Loch K. Johnson

Water Politics
Ken Conca

Business Ethics
John Hooker